CW01618776

Stagnation nation

Navigating a route to a fairer and more prosperous Britain

THE INTERIM REPORT OF
THE ECONOMY 2030 INQUIRY

Acknowledgements

This book was produced with input from across the Resolution Foundation and CEP research teams, and authored by Torsten Bell, Emily Fry, Gavin Kelly, Louise Murphy, Greg Thwaites and Daniel Tomlinson. We would like to thank Mike Brewer, Tania Burchardt, Rui Costa, Swati Dhingra, Steve Machin, Henry Overman, Anna Valero and David Willetts for their contributions over recent months as the argument and content of the book has taken shape. The leadership of the Commissioners and the guidance of the Advisory Group has been invaluable throughout this process, and we are grateful for all that both groups have brought to the work of The Economy 2030 Inquiry to date.

Citation
If you are using this document in your own writing, our preferred citation is: Resolution Foundation & Centre for Economic Performance, LSE, *Stagnation nation: Navigating a route to a fairer and more prosperous Britain,* Resolution Foundation, July 2022

Permission to share
This document is published under the Creative Commons Attribution Non Commercial No Derivatives 3.0 England and Wales Licence. This allows anyone to download, reuse, reprint, distribute, and/or copy Economy 2030 Inquiry publications without written permission subject to the conditions set out in the Creative Commons Licence. For commercial use, please contact: info@resolutionfoundation.org

Cover image
The image used on the front cover of this report was acquired by the Moderate Resolution Imaging Spectroradiometer aboard NASA's Terra satellite. Image credit: NASA and rawpixel.com

The Economy 2030 Inquiry

The UK has great strengths, but is over a decade into a period of stagnation. The toxic combination of slow growth and high inequality was posing challenges for low-to-middle income Britain's living standards even before the post-pandemic cost of living crisis struck. The task of the 2020s is to overcome this stagnation while wrestling with a decade of significant economic change, as Britain recovers from the pandemic, adjusts to exiting the EU, and transitions towards a net zero future.

The Economy 2030 Inquiry, a collaboration between the Resolution Foundation and the Centre for Economic Performance at the London School of Economics, funded by the Nuffield Foundation, is examining this decisive decade, and how Britain can confront the dangers of stagnation to become a stronger and fairer economy.

This Interim Report brings together the first phase of the Inquiry's research, focused on the state of the UK economy and the changes facing it. It draws on that analysis, but also on conversations with citizens and policy makers about their experiences of the country as it is, and aspirations for what it could be. It will give direction to the development of coherent policy proposals that will be the focus of The Inquiry's final report, to be published in 2023.

Contents

Executive summary

Executive summary

The promise of shared prosperity is central to the social contract in modern democracies.

Countries are bound together in a sense of shared endeavour by many things, from a common history to the collective provision of security for our homes, families and communities. But as traditional hierarchies have weakened and advanced economies become more diverse, the role of the state in delivering shared prosperity has become more central in underpinning social contracts. With rising wages, higher employment, the provision of public services or support for those who fall on hard times, the British state and economy have delivered in the past. Real wages nearly quadrupled, while state spending on healthcare as a share of the economy almost trebled, between the Second World War and the turn of the millennium.

But that progress, and the strength it gives to our society and democracy, should not be taken for granted. There are periods when this underpinning of our social contract comes under pressure; when a clear route to a better tomorrow is lacking, the improvements people expect dry up and some groups are left wondering whether the country works for them. Britain in 2022, as we outline in this book, is in this undesirable position.

That promise is under threat. The cost of living crisis is the immediate focus, but our ambitions must extend far beyond simply getting through it

The current cost of living crisis rightly dominates the attention of the public and policy makers, as the highest inflation for 40 years takes a steep toll on household living standards. Double-digit inflation is forecast to arrive later in 2022, but is already a reality for the lowest-income households. **Government support in excess of £30 billion this year will mitigate the impact of rising bills, but will not prevent household incomes falling this year and next**. This is not the recovery from the pandemic anyone was hoping for.

But as pressing as today's issues are, policy makers must lift their sights to broader challenges to ensure our shared prosperity. British households went into this crisis with low levels of financial resilience, and are forecast a sluggish living standards recovery coming out of it: **we're set to take until the middle of this decade to return to pre-pandemic income levels.** This is the result of an economy defined by the low growth of the past 15 years and high inequality of the past four decades, which pose risks not only for our economy, but to our society and democracy too. This makes the UK a stagnation nation.

Britain's huge strengths and talents are not being harnessed: we are 15 years into a period of relative economic decline

We caught up with more-productive countries like France, Germany and the US during the 1990s and early 2000s. But that came to an end in the mid-2000s and our relative performance has been declining ever since. **On the eve of the financial crisis, GDP per capita in the UK was just 6 per cent lower than in Germany, but this gap had risen to 11 per cent by 2019.** Our GDP performance would have been even weaker were it not for strong employment growth, with hours worked having increased by more than two-and-a-half times the rate in France (11 per cent compared to 4 per cent).

This reflects a productivity slowdown far surpassing those seen in similar economies. **Labour productivity grew by just 0.4 per cent a year in the UK in the 12 years following the financial crisis, half the rate of the 25 richest OECD countries (0.9 per cent).** Having almost caught up with the economies of France and Germany from the 1990s to the mid-2000s, the UK's productivity gap with them has almost tripled since 2008 from 6 per cent to 16 per cent – equivalent to an extra £3,700 in lost output per person.

Claims that these measures of economic progress mean little for ordinary workers are common but painfully wide of the mark. Weak productivity growth has fed directly into flatlining wages and sluggish income growth: **real wages grew by an average of 33 per cent a decade from 1970 to 2007, but this fell to below zero in the 2010s.** The result is that by 2018, typical household incomes were 16 per cent lower in the UK than in Germany and 9 per cent lower than in France, having been higher in 2007.

Gaps between people and places are too high – the UK has the highest income inequality of any major European economy

While Britons have been living with low wages for the last 15 years, inequality has been a problem for more than twice as long. Having surged during the 1980s, and remained consistently high ever since, **income inequality in the UK was higher than any other large European country in 2018.** This is not a league table we should be aiming to top.

The persistence of income inequality comes despite the success of the National Minimum Wage in reducing hourly wage inequality between the bottom and the middle. This reflects the top (largely men) continuing to pull away from the middle, lower earners working shorter hours and housing costs rising for poorer households even as interest rate falls boost living standards at the top.

Income and productivity gaps between places both matter, and in the UK both are high and persistent. **Income per person in the richest local authority – Kensington and Chelsea (£52,500) – was 4.5 times that of the poorest – Nottingham (£11,700) – in 2019**.

Meanwhile, 80 per cent of the income variation between areas we see today is explained by the differences back in 1997. And productivity disparities are larger still, with that between the leading city and potential high-performing others greater than in peer countries such as France. For example, **London is 41 per cent more productive than Manchester whereas Paris is 26 per cent more productive than Lyon.**

Low growth and high inequality are a toxic combination. When sustained they are a disaster for low-to-middle income Britain and the young in particular

The twin challenges that Britain faces – low growth and high inequality – are substantial issues on their own, but together they create a toxic combination.

Slow growth is always a problem, but even more so when lower-income households lack financial resilience: over one-in-four adults went into the pandemic saying they would not be able to manage on their savings for a month if their income stopped. Inequality seems to matter more when the economic music stops: the share of the public citing poverty and inequality as one of the most important issues facing the country rose from 7 per cent in 2010 to 19 per cent pre-pandemic.

This toxic combination is a disaster for low-to-middle income Britain and younger generations. We might think of ourselves as a country on a par with France and Germany, but we need to recognise that, except for those at the top, this is simply no longer true when it comes to living standards.

Low-income households in the UK are now 22 per cent poorer than their counterparts in France, and 21 per cent poorer than low-income households in Germany. It's important to comprehend just how material these gaps are: the living standards of the lowest-income households in the UK are £3,800 lower than their French equivalents. Meanwhile the young have seen generational pay progress grind to a halt and **those born in the early 1980s were almost half as likely to own their own home as the cohort born in the early 1950s at age 30**. We cannot go on like this.

The 2020s will be a decisive decade of change, reinforcing rather than resolving stagnation

Countries can go through phases of relative stability, but the UK in the 2020s will not be such a country. Long-standing demographic and technological shifts will continue and combine with Brexit, the aftermath of Covid-19 and the net zero transition. These will bring significant disruption for some, but not the radical reset for our economy or large job losses many predict. Instead, rather than solving our stagnation, change risks reinforcing it.

Brexit has already brought change, albeit not always in the form widely expected. Foreign direct investment has held up since the referendum and 18 months in to our new trading relationship it is not clear our exports to the EU have fallen disproportionately. Instead the UK has suffered a broad-based fall in both openness and competitiveness. **Between 2019 and 2021, UK trade openness fell by 8 percentage points** (compared to a 2 percentage point decline in France). The UK also lost market share across three of its largest non-EU goods import markets in 2021: the US, Canada, and Japan.

More change is to come as some sectors serving the EU market shrink and others grow as a result of less competition domestically. Fishing output will fall by 30 per cent, while food manufacturing could increase by more than 5 per cent. But these changes will not lead to the benefits some hoped for: a manufacturing revival or more regionally-balanced economy. UK manufacturing will change rather than grow, as high-productivity sectors like chemicals and electronics shrink even as lower-productivity food manufacturing expands. **Wages in London, Wales and the North East will be hardest hit by the trade impact of leaving the EU on productivity which, across the country as a whole, means workers will be £470 worse off by the end of the decade.**

Covid-19 caused huge changes to our economy and our lives. But just as collections of face coverings no longer pile up in people's homes, so too many of the economic shifts wrought by the pandemic have unwound. The online share of retail spending shot up from 20 per cent to 38 per cent mid-pandemic, but has fallen back to 27 per cent in the latest data - only 4 percentage points above the pre-crisis trend.

Working from home has persisted for higher earners (the proportion of people who reported that they worked from home on a regular basis surged during the pandemic, and remains high at 38 per cent of all workers in early 2022) but shows no signs of living up to claims that it would transform our economic geography or our productivity.

Instead, the pandemic has provided new headwinds to output: **there are 430,000 fewer people in work now than pre-pandemic** and **investment remains more than 9 per cent below its pre-pandemic level**. It's also, of course, been part of the inflation surge we are now all living through. If anyone ever thought that a global pandemic would bring big silver linings to our shores, they should think again.

The net zero transition brings opportunities as well as change for workers and costs for consumers. But it is not a silver bullet for the UK economy

The net zero transition is crucial to not just the planet, but in making the UK a greener and healthier place to live. But it comes with challenges in the here and now. This won't be in the form of large-scale job losses, with job change rather than destruction the norm. For example, **24 per cent of those**

working in emissions-intensive 'brown' jobs are large goods vehicle drivers – whose jobs will not disappear even as the vehicles they use become greener.

Instead major disruption will be felt by people as consumers, as our net zero commitments require significant investment in low-carbon infrastructure that has to be paid for. In the 2020s, this is principally about making our homes more energy efficient.

Here there is a risk of outright failure to accelerate the transition, which has stalled after **a 90 per cent fall in insulation installations since 2013 even as the Government's net zero strategy suggests we will be upgrading a million homes per year by 2030.** If we remain on track, the challenge facing policy makers will be to ensure the costs are fairly born: **72 per cent of low-income homeowners live in poorly insulated homes that will cost over £8,000 to bring up to standard – almost as much as their average disposable income of £9,100.**

The concrete questions of how these investments will be paid for should receive more attention than misplaced claims that net zero is a silver bullet that will hugely boost, or a catastrophe that will hold back, growth. There are new opportunities to be seized and green innovations to be exploited, but during the 2020s the main impact of the net zero transition on GDP will be to change its composition, as we invest more but consume less, rather than its level.

These changes are not the answers to the toxic combination of low growth and high inequality – they are the context within which the badly-needed attempt to renew the country's path to economic success needs to be placed.

We cannot go on like this. The task of the 2020s is to renew the UK's economic strategy and end stagnation

Relying on supposed silver linings or silver bullets is part of a wider problem: the belief that a policy shift in one area holds the answer to stagnation. It won't. Instead the task for the 2020s is to renew the UK's economic strategy – its route to shared economic success.

Why is a strategy needed? First, because the challenges are large and have been sustained. **8 million younger Brits have never worked in an economy that has sustained rising average wages, while 25 million have never lived in a country where the top 10 per cent have had incomes less than five times that of the bottom 10 per cent**.

Second, because those challenges and the change to come are inter-dependent. And third because the financial crisis and Brexit have blown up major components of the UK's long-standing approach, which had itself been found wanting given the large and persistent gaps between people and places.

Important elements of a more comprehensive approach are visible, from the UK Government's focus on science, to the Labour Party's green investment plans, or the Welsh Government's prioritisation of social partnership. But the test for a broader economic strategy is that it requires: **goal orientation**, being clear about the problem a strategy is trying to solve; **clarity about context**, understanding the type of country we are and the opportunities and constraints this brings, without nostalgia about the past or wishful thinking about the future; **realism about trade offs**, recognising the tensions that always exist in setting strategy; policies of **sufficient scale** to plausibly move the dial; and, finally, **staying power,** because change takes time and short-termism has been a key weakness of the UK throughout the 20th century.

No one believes that Britain has such a strategy guiding policy making and shaping private decision taking today and there is a recognition, from the Chancellor downwards, that we cannot continue as we are. But a growing consensus about the problem is very different to being serious about the solution. Some argue we don't need growth because it won't translate into gains for ordinary households, ignoring the reality that a lack of growth is the cause of flatlining wages. More common is to recognise that growth is necessary, or that inequality is too high, but to be deeply unserious about what it might take to change things. The realities of modern Britain are regularly ignored and the trade offs between different objectives wished away. We are short-term to our core.

Understanding your country is a prerequisite for making a success of it: Britain is a services superpower

Not being serious begins at the most fundamental level: failing to understand what Britain's 21st century economy actually looks like. Commentators often talk of the British economy as being narrowly built on banking, which is as misplaced as the claim that there is an easy route to turning ourselves into a German-style manufacturing superpower

These pop narratives obscure the reality that Britain is a broad-based services economy, built on successful musicians and architects as well as bankers. We're about ICT, culture and marketing, as well as finance (whose fraction of total exports fell from 12 per cent in 9 per cent in the pre-pandemic decade). No one celebrates it, but **the UK is the second largest exporter of services in the world**. And our services specialism does not lie behind our recent underperformance: on average, services-led economies tend to be richer than manufacturing-driven ones. It is also perfectly consistent with rapid export growth: global demand actually grew faster in our key export industries than in China's in the decade to 2019, but China's exports grew twice as fast.

We have manufacturing strengths too: pharmaceuticals, aerospace and beverages stand out. But the services-led nature of our economy is not going away. The things countries are good at are highly persistent: of the top 10 products the UK was most specialised in back in 1989, seven were in our top 10 in 2019. Even Brexit, the biggest shake-up to our economic place in the world in decades, will have little impact on the balance between services and manufacturing.

Recognising the nature of our economy is not the same thing as welcoming all aspects of it, but an economic strategy that fails to understand it is no strategy at all. It will leave us without a clear view of how growth is achieved, exposed to policy mistakes, and failing to address the challenges being a services-led economy brings: upward pressure on inequality between people and places. **Jobs in tradable services are 80 per cent more likely than average to pay in the top 5 per cent while services exports are concentrated in the highest-wage areas.** Wrestling with this is essential, and possible. France is services focused like us but has much lower inequality

Fundamentally we need to recognise that the path to future prosperity lies in being a better version of Britain, not a British version of Germany.

Britain's big cities outside London succeeding is the route to higher national income and lower regional gaps. But it requires change on a scale not currently contemplated

While our current economic specialisation is consistent with future prosperity, our regional divides are not. The large productivity divide between the Greater South East and the rest of the UK squeezes the brakes on economic progress nationally and accelerates regional income gaps.

Recognising the services-led nature of our economy tells us what a plausible path to releasing this brake will be. High-value services industries thrive when similar firms co-locate in large places with highly-educated populations: cities. Indeed, **the importance of an area's workforce size, skill levels, and stocks of capital (including intangibles) in determining its productivity has grown during the 21st century.** But far too few of our big cities, all deeply scarred by deindustrialisation, have successfully made the transition to a services economy: **all of England's biggest cities outside London have productivity levels below the national average.**

Focusing on turning this around would turn levelling up from rhetoric into the core of a renewed economic strategy. And, given the geography of our islands, it is not a minority concern. The UK may be a 'green and pleasant land', but **69 per cent of the UK population live in cities or their hinterlands, compared to 56 per cent in France and just 40 per cent in Italy.**

Progress is possible, building on signs of success: **between 1997 and 2015, Leeds grew the share of its output accounted for by business services from below the national average to well above it.** But we shouldn't shy away from the fact that turning more cities into services superpowers isn't going to be easy. The level of investment required is simply huge. Halving Manchester's productivity gap to London, so that it becomes as productive as Edinburgh, would require tens of billions of pounds of investment and an increase in size of over 500,000 workers. Change on that scale is needed but inconsistent with national politicians refusing to concentrate efforts or local politicians unable to embrace the disruption involved because they lack the powers to shape it.

As well as recognising the benefits this approach could bring – closing regional productivity and income gaps, and raising national income – we must also be clear about the challenges it raises. People will need connecting to the new opportunities and housing policy must respond to avoid the big winners being existing owners of land. The goal is more successful cities, not clones of London with low earners facing high housing costs.

This has to be a high investment decade – requiring more change for the private than public sector

The 2020s has to be a high -investment decade not just because of net zero, but because the UK has been a low-investment economy for too long. **In the 40 years to 2019, total fixed investment in the UK averaged 19 per cent of GDP, the lowest in the G7**. This may have made sense when the UK was the most advanced economy in the world with a huge capital stock advantage over its competitors, but it's a recipe for relative decline today.

The public sector has started to turn the corner. Despite being the focus of political debate on investment it is no longer where the big problem is. **After decades of underinvestment the government has now increased public sector net investment to its highest sustained levels since the 1970s.**

Instead, the private sector is where the challenge lies. **Business investment was only 10 per cent of GDP in 2019, far behind an average of 13 per cent in France, Germany and the USA**. Investment growth stalled after the Brexit referendum and has recovered slowly from Covid-19 – while GDP has returned to pre-pandemic levels, business investment remains 9 per cent down.

Stepping back, our analysis has shown that **persistent low investment means virtually all of the productivity gap with France is explained by French workers having more capital to work with.**

Creativity will be required to turn this situation around. The Chancellor is rightly examining what more the tax system can do, but there are limits to the role of traditional tax incentives, which struggle to cover most intangible investment, in an economy like the UK's. Ending the country's entrenched and pervasive low-investment culture will be key, as will delivering greater economic stability. The latter is obviously made harder by repeated shocks, but our failure to reform our macroeconomic framework for an era of low interest rates risks it being harder to respond to them adequately. We should not forget that highest investment will also come with trade offs in the form of lower consumption or higher borrowing from abroad.

Greater investment in human capital, where progress has slowed and outcomes are very unequal, is also needed. With the quantity of labour falling post-pandemic, we need to focus on its quality. This runs from school, where the gap in numeracy skills between 16-20-year-olds who do not have a parent that attained an upper-secondary qualification (A-level equivalent) and those that did is the third largest in the OECD, to the workplace, where **the average number of days an employee spends in training each year has fallen by 18 per cent (from 7.8 per cent to 6.4 per cent) between 2011 and 2017.**

Rather than address these issues our policy debates focus on the question of whether we are doing too much education or fears of a brain drain from poorer place, despite **young people from the most-deprived areas being two-and-a-half times less likely to leave their home area upon reaching adulthood than their peers in the least-deprived quintile.**

We need to think harder about change – how we help workers manage it and whether our economy has too little of it

The 2020s may see an acceleration of labour market change as the shocks and transitions discussed above play out. We must do a better job than we have in the past to help workers losing their jobs. On average, **in the UK, 40 per cent of employed people experience a large loss of income when becoming non-employed, compared to 30 per cent of employed people in Germany and 26 per cent of employed people in France.**

But taking economic change seriously also means ignoring popular claims that it is permanently speeding up, when it's actually been slowing down: **the reallocation of labour between sectors was equivalent to 7 per cent of total employment in in the decade to 2021, hugely down on the 20 per cent experienced in the 1980s.** Any reversal of the downward trend this decade will not be large enough to return us to the highs of decades past.

Indeed, an economic strategy for the 2020s needs to go further and confront the worrying lack of 'good change' seen in the UK in recent years. **The proportion of workers switching job each quarter declined by 25 per cent between 2000 and 2019 despite those moving jobs typically enjoying pay growth 4 percentage points higher than individuals staying put.**

Part of this looks to be a product of people being reluctant to take labour market risks given the lack of income insurance offered by the UK's welfare state: workers need both a cushion against job loss and a secure platform from which to embrace good change. Housing costs rising faster in higher-paying areas has also locked people out of opportunities. Lower labour market dynamism is a problem for reallocating workers to higher-productivity firms, something that is much more important to raising national productivity than policy makers current focus on supporting the 'long tail' of low-productivity firms.

A serious economic strategy will be as hard-headed about lower inequality as it is about higher growth

Success for Britain does not look like becoming America. Despite being far richer, the past decade has shown the dangers to democracy from being the most unequal advanced economy in the world. And there is nothing economically or democratically sustainable about a UK status quo that saw **the number of families experiencing destitution reach 1 million in 2019, an increase of one-third compared to 2017**. So we must be just as serious about reducing inequality as boosting growth.

But that is not where we are today. Businesses think it's enough to talk about environmental, social and governance (ESG) issues; we get local authorities to bid for small pots of cash as our answer to gaping regional divides; and each new crisis sees us patching up the welfare state rather than ensuring it is fit for purpose in the first place.

Good jobs must be a central objective of a renewed economic strategy

The UK's high employment rate is a strength we should not take for granted; **the poorest half of households experienced two-thirds of the jobs growth in**

the decade after the financial crisis. But celebrating the strengths of our flexible labour market has too often prevented us from being serious about tackling its problems.

Indefensibly, **half of shift workers in Britain receive less than a week's notice of their working hours or schedules.** While higher-paid workers have seen their exposure to insecure forms of work fall, low earners have not and are around three times more likely to experience contract insecurity or volatile hours or pay. The minimum wage has driven the first sustained falls in low hourly pay for four decades, but far less progress has been made in reducing inequality in weekly wages.

Jobs with decent pay and conditions underpin any path to widely shared prosperity. Politicians' promises that all jobs will be available everywhere are very far from serious, but ensuring good jobs exist in every part of our country – including in the non-tradable sectors that provide largely for the domestic market, from care to hospitality – must be a central objective of an economic strategy rather than a by-product of it.

We need to be less enamoured of the status quo and more open to policy innovations. The minimum wage has hugely raised earnings without the job losses many predicted, yet we still underestimate the degree of choice we have over the quality of work, particularly in sectors not exposed to international competition. Yes, higher pay and better conditions will bring trade offs, including higher prices. But this shouldn't deter us from such an approach. **Countries with higher prices tend to have lower inequality.**

As well as getting the basics right in terms of labour market regulation and enforcement, Britain should learn lessons from bolder approaches to labour market innovation taking place in similar Anglo-Saxon labour markets like New Zealand and focus on the quality of work in growing occupations that exist in every community – like care and retrofitting.

There is a lot to play for. The focus today is on the combination of high inflation and a tight labour market leading to industrial disputes, but structural questions of power in the labour market matter more for pay levels and inequality in the long-term. **Under 10 per cent of low-paid private sector workers are unionised**, and the decline of unions explains a sixth of the increase in wage inequality among men between 1983 and 2019. Looking across the whole labour market, **wages could be as much as 15 per cent**

lower than they would otherwise be because of a lack of worker power, equivalent to almost £100 a week for the average worker.

Places are different, but everywhere should be a good place to live

The Government's 'Levelling Up' agenda has been criticised for focusing on liveability, rather than just productivity. But it is the right call to focus on both. Productivity in 21st century Britain will be unevenly distributed across the country, but the status of the places in which we live and the standard of their public realm should not be. Our qualitative research showed a consistent focus from people on the state of town centres, the quality and availability of public services and the capacity of local government to deliver the basics. **The share of people thinking their local area has deteriorated in the preceding two years rose from 20 per cent in 2013-14 to 26 per cent in 2019-20.**

Tackling this sense of decline is essential to delivering on a social contract that promises you'll gain from the national economy wherever you live. But Britain is not serious, yet, about delivering this. **A striking 18 per cent of all revenue grants and 30 per cent of all capital grants for local authorities are wound up every year, hindering long-term planning.** And council revenues per person fell by 30 per cent between 2009 and 2019 in the most-deprived places, compared to 15 per cent in the least-deprived places.

Ensuring that poorer areas remain well-funded creates a clear trade off with the imperative noted above for greater devolution, required to underpin strong local economic leadership. Powers to raise more taxes locally inevitably give more fiscal flexibility to richer areas. But other, less-centralised, countries manage this trade off, and the UK must too.

The burden for funding a growing state can't all be shouldered by the young

The exact size of the state in the years ahead depends on political choices, but the 2020s are best thought of as an era of a bigger government than we were used to in the 2010s. An ageing society, rising costs of healthcare, and new demands such as the pandemic's legacy all point in that direction. The approaches by which pressures for a bigger welfare state have been absorbed in decades gone by are also not available. **Defence spending was**

reduced from 8 per cent of GDP in the mid-20th century to around 2 per cent today as health and education spending grew, but the Prime Minister is now calling for an increase to 2.5 per cent of GDP.

When combined with low growth this explains why the same politicians declaring their low-tax 'instincts' have raised taxes to their highest levels since the 1940s. But the elevated level of taxes has not prompted sufficient focus on good taxes. Both main parties have in recent decades focused tax rises on National Insurance, despite it falling narrowly on younger workers at a time of flatlining wages. Take the recent Health and Social Care Levy: **a typical 25-year-old worker today will pay an extra £12,600 over their working life from the employee part of the tax rise alone, compared to nothing for landlords and most pensioners.**

A strategy for the 2020s will need to consider new approaches, recognising that **wealth has risen from three to almost eight times national income since the 1980s, while wealth taxes have not risen at all as a share of GDP.**

A decent society doesn't allow those in need to fall ever further behind the rest of society

The UK has deliberately chosen incredibly low levels of basic income protection in our social security system, prioritising spending instead on the extra costs of children and housing. The long duration of this approach however has completely decoupled some of the poorest households' incomes from the rest of society: **the basic level of benefits is now just £77 per week – only 13 per cent of average pay and its lowest level on record.**

Large families and disabled people are falling behind, with almost one-third (31 per cent) of households with a disabled adult being in poverty in 2019-20, compared to 19 per cent of families in which no one has a disability. And **pre-pandemic almost half of families with three or more children were in poverty, up from one-third in 2012-13.** Any economic strategy that claims to be serious about reducing inequality and financial hardship will need to take a different approach.

Slow growth and high inequality are far from inevitable. Progress on both would transform the lives of low-to-middle income Britain

So there is a lot to be done to renew the UK's economic strategy and it will be far from easy, economically or politically. Some might question how achievable a material increase in growth or reduction in inequality is for a relatively small and mature economy like the UK, taking the view that these difficulties outweigh the potential benefits. They might point to arguments about slowing growth at the global frontier. But accepting such fatalism misjudges the room for improvement the UK has, because we are not at the head of the pack. It also too lightly passes over the transformational impact plausible progress would have for low-to-middle income households.

Progress is possible for the UK for one big reason: we have a lot of room to catch up towards both the prosperity and inequality frontiers. To see why consider a set of similar comparator economies to the UK: Australia, Canada, France, Germany, and the Netherlands. These are not the richest, or most equal, countries in the world and we would long have considered them our peers. But **we're now 21 per cent poorer than these countries on average**, demonstrating copious amounts of catch-up potential that dwarfs the Office for Budget Responsibility's forecast of a 4 per cent hit to our long-run productivity from Brexit, relative to remaining in the EU.

These countries are also more equal than the UK: **if we reduced inequality to the levels in the comparison group, it would raise incomes for the poorest fifth of the country by more than 20 per cent,** while reducing them for the richest in society.

If we were able to close the gap in income and inequality with the average of this group it would have huge effects, increasing incomes by over 40 per cent among the poorest fifth of the country, and around one third for the middle, without reducing incomes at the top (indeed, they would still rise slightly).

This is not to say this is precisely where Britain could end up, but to demonstrate the size of the prize available. A better future for the UK does not need global growth to suddenly accelerate, or Britain to match American levels of productivity and Scandinavian levels of inequality. It just requires us to have the resolve to do what is necessary to converge with similar countries who, in the scheme of things, are not so very different to us. There is a lot to play for, especially for those on low-to-middle incomes.

Towards a fairer and more prosperous Britain

This book brings together an analysis of the key challenges facing the UK and the strengths that can be brought to bear in addressing them. It outlines the contours of an economic strategy that could provide a plausible path to confronting stagnation, focusing on the most material elements of the route. We have not covered off every policy area or prescribed the relevance of this national approach to devolved or sub-national administrations, whose own strategies will also have to wrestle with significant variation across the country.

This book comes at the mid-point of The Economy 2030 Inquiry. The second phase of the project will assess how policy can make a reality of such a strategy, a subject on which others will have many views to contribute. The prize is reviving the promise of shared prosperity that underpins our social contract, and the route to it is a renewed economic strategy that helps guide Britain through the 2020s and beyond to a richer, fairer, and greener future.

Stagnation nation: 10 key facts

1. Low growth: real wages grew by 33 per cent a decade from 1970 to 2007 on average, but this fell to below zero in the 2010s.
2. High inequality: income inequality in the UK was higher than any other large European country in 2018.
3. The toxic combination: low-income households in the UK are 22 per cent poorer than their counterparts in France, and typical household incomes are 9 per cent lower.
4. Stalled progress: 8 million young workers have never worked in an economy with sustained average wage rises, and those born in the early 1980s were almost half as likely to own a home as those born in the early 1950s at age 30.
5. Levelling up: income per person in the richest local authority – Kensington and Chelsea (£52,500) – was over 4 times that of the poorest – Nottingham (£11,700) – in 2019.
6. Brexit Britain: fishing output could shrink by 30 per cent by 2030 as a result of Brexit, but food and beverages manufacturing output could increase by more than 5 per cent.
7. The nature of our economy: Britain is the second largest exporter of services in the world, behind only the US.
8. Good work: half of shift workers in Britain receive less than a week's notice of their working hours or schedules.
9. Staying put: Young people from the most-deprived areas are two-and-a-half times less likely to leave their home area upon reaching adulthood than their peers in the least-deprived places.
10. Burden sharing: wealth has risen from three to almost eight times national income since the 1980s, but wealth taxes have flatlined as a share of GDP.

Introduction

Britain 2022: stepping out of a pandemic into a cost of living crisis

In 2022 the UK was meant to have started on the road to recovery following the ravages of Covid-19. Instead, our anxious focus on fast-rising case rates has, almost instantaneously, been replaced by one on surging prices: the first global pandemic in 100 years has been followed by the arrival of inflation not seen for four decades. Inflation has risen from close to zero at the start of 2021 to 9.1 per cent in May 2022, consistently surprising official forecasters (see Figure 1).

Figure 1: The Bank of England is forecasting the highest inflation in 40 years

Annual CPI inflation: outturn and various Bank of England forecasts

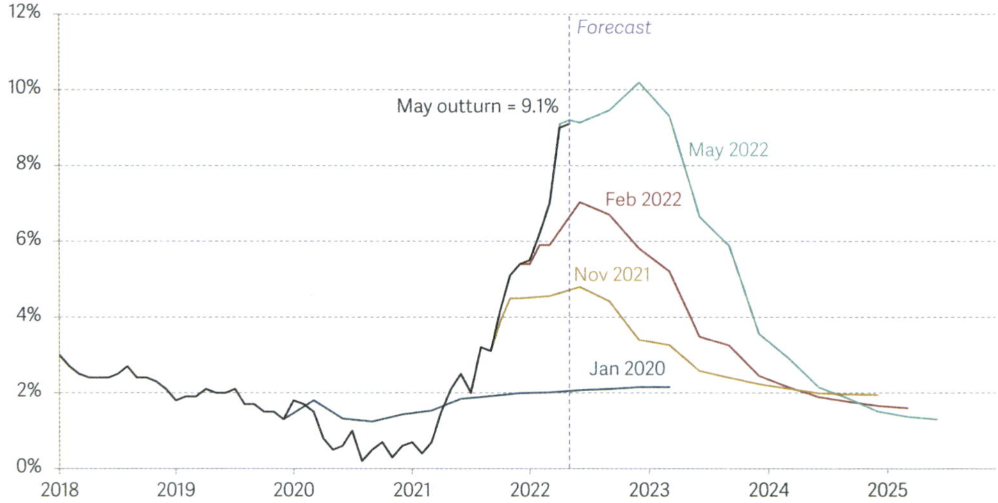

Source: Bank of England, Monetary Policy Report, various; ONS, Consumer Price Inflation.

The squeeze on living standards this brings is bad for everyone, but it is particularly punishing for low-to-middle income households. The double-digit inflation that will shortly arrive in the UK is already a reality for the poorest households who face an inflation rate at least 1.6 percentage points higher than the richest households.[1] This is because the current price surge is driven by energy price hikes the likes of which no one born after the mid-1970s has experienced before, combined with the fact that poor households spend more than three times as much on gas and electricity bills as a proportion of expenditure than the rest of society.[2] This threatens a catastrophe for household living standards and poses a severe test for policy makers in both HM Treasury and the Bank of England. The unequal impact of high inflation is of concern to people in the UK, as we heard in recent focus groups.[3]

> *"I think if everybody's making sacrifices, if everybody's going to pay more for electricity, pay more for fuel, we should all feel the pinch. ... It always seems to be the people on the lowest incomes, the people who are working-class, that's having to struggle."*
>
> (Focus group participant, Paisley)

Surging inflation is rightly policy makers' top priority

The scale and nature of these price rises means that European governments have stepped in to provide significant support to households. In the UK this support has delayed the feedthrough of wholesale energy price rises into household energy bills (via the energy price cap), directly subsidised everyone's energy bills, and provided significant income support to poorer households. This has come at a cost of well over £30 billion this year.[4]

While fiscal policy has focused on ameliorating the impact of price rises already in train, monetary policy makers have been wrestling with how to prevent rising inflation from becoming embedded in the UK economy. A faster than expected labour market recovery, and some signs of emerging wage pressure, has led to the first material tightening in monetary policy since before the financial crisis, with interest rates increasing by 1.15 percentage points between December 2021 and June 2022 to reach the highest level in 13

---

1 Analysis of ONS, Consumer Prices; ONS, Living Costs and Food Survey.

2 ONS, Energy prices and their effect on households, February 2022.

3 The quotes used throughout this book come from two recent reports: K Handscomb, L Judge & H Slaughter, Listen up: Individual experiences of work, consumption and society, Resolution Foundation, May 2022; L Judge & D Tomlinson, All over the place: Perspectives on local economic prosperity, Resolution Foundation, June 2022.

4 T Bell et al., Back on target: Analysis of the Government's additional cost of living support, Resolution Foundation, May 2022.

years.[5] Managing the impact of inflation on families and firms, and attempting to cool the labour market without causing a recession, will remain the immediate priorities for policy makers in the months ahead. Neither is going to be easy.

The £15 billion of additional support for households announced in May 2022 will provide significant help to households in 2022. But, as Figure 2 shows, even after accounting for this intervention, the latest Bank of England forecasts suggest that household incomes are still set to be 1.8 per cent lower in 2022 than in 2021, and to remain below their mid-pandemic 2020 levels as late as 2024

Figure 2: Household incomes could still fall by 1.8 per cent in 2022, even after additional cost of living support

Outturn and projections for real household disposable income per person: UK

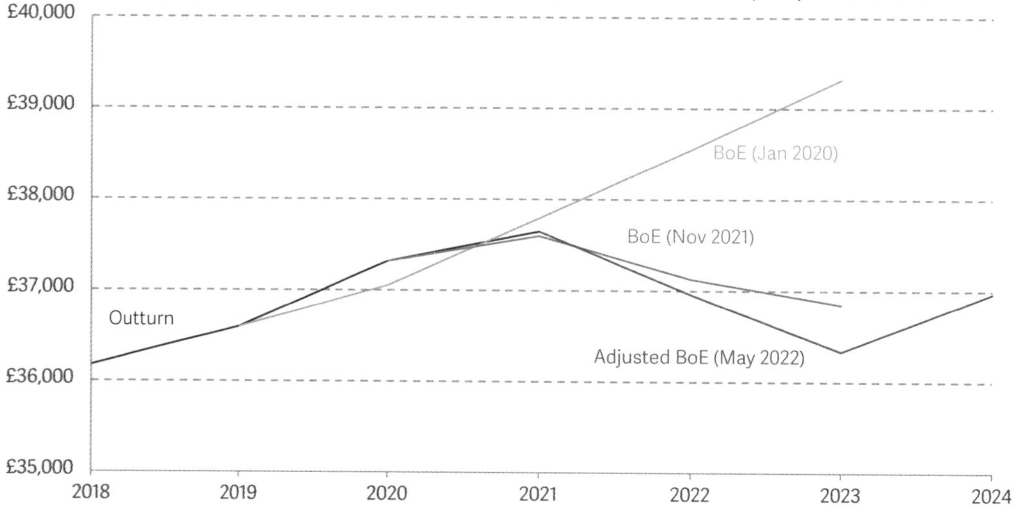

Notes: Bank of England (BoE) forecasts. May 2022 forecast adjusted for the additional support for households announced by the Government in May 2022. Includes non-profit institutions serving households (NPISH).
Source: ONS, National Accounts; Bank of England, Monetary Policy Report, May 2022; HM Treasury, Cost of living support factsheet: 26 May 2022.

5 www.bankofengland.co.uk/boeapps/database/Bank-Rate, accessed 23 June 2022.

But the rest of the 2020s will need to be about far more than responding to this latest crisis

Getting back to where we were, incomes wise, in the middle of the pandemic cannot be the limit of our ambitions. The very reason British households, particularly those on lower incomes, have so little resilience in the face of surging energy bills is the lack of meaningful living standards growth in the UK since the mid-2000s combined with high inequality inherited from earlier decades. For 15 years the UK has bumped from crisis to crisis – sometimes improvising successfully in the face of them, but with each period of turbulence adding to our problems and distracting attention from how deep they run. As a result, existing economic debates and policy mindsets all too often fail to reflect the scale of the challenge the country faces.

So if the priority for 2022 is to respond to the cost of living crisis, our ambition for the 2020s should instead be to rebuild the UK's path to economic success. That will require a vision for how the country can improve and a practical plan for making that vision a reality: in short, the UK needs to renew its economic strategy.

This isn't about abstract utopias but a hard-headed assessment of what a plausibly successful economic strategy could look like. This view must be grounded in a clear analysis of where we start from – our strengths as well as weaknesses – and an understanding of the change we already know is coming during the course of the 2020s. Providing those twin assessments, and exploring the route forward for the UK's economy in light of them, is the purpose of this short book.

Throughout, we draw on the detailed research carried out to-date as part of The Economy 2030 Inquiry, a collaboration between the Resolution Foundation and the Centre for Economic Performance at the London School for Economics, funded by the Nuffield Foundation.[6] Our focus is the strategy for the UK economy as a whole. However, the increasingly devolved nature of governance means the project should be of interest to (and indeed is informed by the work of) national and sub-regional administrations who will pursue a variety of approaches within any UK-wide economic strategy.

6 All research of The Economy 2030 Inquiry is available at www.economy2030.resolutionfoundation.org.

We proceed as follows:

- **Chapter One** examines the UK's combination of long-term slow growth and high inequality, which defined the nation as it entered the 2020s.
- **Chapter Two** turns to the change that Brexit, Covid-19, technology, demography, and the net zero transition will bring to the UK economy during this decade.
- **Chapter Three** argues that a renewal of our economic strategy is urgently required and that, despite signs of progress on some specific components, there is currently little evidence of a new and overarching approach emerging.
- **Chapter Four** explores what a plausible economic strategy for the UK might look like. We do not provide a comprehensive survey of all of economic and social policy, but focus in on the most important constraints, trade-offs, and opportunities that policy makers, and the nation as whole, face.
- **Chapter Five** addresses directly the question of whether it is realistic to expect that a mature economy like the UK can do much better than it currently is, recognising some of the shared challenges weighing on growth across advanced societies.

Some may argue this approach overstates the potential for policy makers to shift the dial on economic performance (although those same people often contend that politicians have made things significantly worse). The task is extremely challenging, but policy can make a major difference for the better: poorer households are much more likely to be able to pay their energy bills this winter because the Chancellor has provided more support, while the minimum wage has resulted in pay growth among the lowest earners running at approaching twice the level of the rest of the workforce over recent decades (something many said could not be done without huge job losses).[7]

7 Since the financial crisis, the median year-on-year wage growth across all workers has averaged approximately 2.6 per cent, whereas the equivalent growth for minimum-wage workers has been 4.5 per cent. For further discussion of pay growth and the impact of the minimum wage, see: N Cominetti et al., Low Pay Britain 2022: Low pay and insecurity in the UK labour market, Resolution Foundation, May 2022.

The UK has also seen periods of significantly improved relative economic performance compared to similar countries within living memory. There is nothing inevitable about our current relative decline, just as there is no automatic reason for why it should end. But the UK should take heart from the fact that it still has underlying economic strengths that should serve it well as it navigates the 2020s, and from the significant political consensus that exists (and which eludes some other advanced economies) around key planks of what needs to be achieved: whether it is closing entrenched regional gaps or the imperative of the net zero transition.

Fatalism, as much as complacency, is the enemy of clear thought about the country's future. Realism, twinned with a sense of informed optimism about the power of policy to improve outcomes over time, will serve us better in facing up to the imperative of restoring rising living standards and making us a more equal country.

Addressing the UK's challenges will strengthen our democracy as well as our economy

Improved economic performance is far from just about economics. Indeed the case for policy makers raising their sights from the already significant challenges of 2022 is that doing so is relevant to the health of our democracy, not just our economy.

Countries are bound together in a sense of shared endeavour by many things – a common history and culture, protection against external enemies abroad and security at home. But as traditional hierarchies have weakened and advanced economies become more diverse, the role of the state in delivering shared prosperity has come to play a greater role in underpinning the social contracts that bind populations, and their government, together. That could be via rising wages, higher employment, the provision of public services or in support provided to those who fall on hard times. The British state and economy have delivered in the past: real wages nearly quadrupled between the Second World War and end of the millennium, while state spending on healthcare almost trebled from 2 to 5 per cent of GDP over the same time period.

But there are periods when the promise of shared prosperity, which underpins our social contract, comes under pressure. When a clear route to a better future is lacking, tensions rise in society, politics becomes more zero sum and the chances of more extreme instability or backsliding from democracy mount.

The UK is not near that situation today, but no-one should take lightly the risks of what can come tomorrow.

And it is perfectly possible that we will end the 2020s with the country being significantly fairer, more productive, greener, and healthier than it is today. So, even as today's cost of living crisis rages, we must recognise the wider challenges and lift our sights to what can be achieved by answering them. That is what this book aims to help us to do.

Chapter One

Stagnation nation

Chapter summary

- The UK economy has huge strengths, from high employment to world class universities.
- But, having grown more quickly than most advanced economies from the 1990s to the mid-2000s, the UK has been in relative decline ever since: the average productivity gap with France, Germany and the US nearly doubled, to 16 per cent, between 2008 and 2019.
- Slow growth is the cause of Britain's flatlining wages: real wages grew by an average of 33 per cent a decade from 1970 to 2007, but this fell to below zero in the 2010s. By 2018 typical household incomes were 16 per cent lower in the UK than in Germany and 9 per cent lower than in France, having been higher in 2007.
- Having surged during the 1980s, and remained consistently high ever since, income inequality in the UK was higher than any other large European country in 2018. Inequality between places is high and persistent too.
- This is stagnation: the toxic combination of low growth and high inequality. It is ruinous for low-to-middle income Britons. Low-income households in the UK are 22 per cent poorer than their counterparts in France, meaning their living standards are £3,800 a year lower than their French equivalents'.
- The young have also lost out: 8 million younger workers have never worked in an economy with sustained average wage rises, and those born in the early 1980s were almost half as likely to own a home as those born in the early 1950s at age 30.
- Stagnation leaves public services struggling, even as the tax burden rises: taxes are on course to reach their highest share of GDP since the 1940s.

The country wrestling with today's cost of living crisis, like the people, places, and firms experiencing it, has a history. Understanding where that has left the UK is the purpose of this chapter. Alongside many strengths, it argues that the Britain of the 2020s risks being defined by the combination of sustained low growth and longer-lasting high inequality. Each brings challenges, but a prolonged period of the two together risks continued stagnation, which should be the priority of policy makers to reverse.

Britain has many advantages and its economy has many strengths

The UK is a privileged and prosperous country in a global context. Having been one of the world's richest countries for several centuries, our national incomes now average 6 per cent above the typical Organisation for Economic Co-operation and Development (OECD) country and our employment rate is high. Setting up a company is easy in the UK, and the adoption of technology among the population is generally swift.

The UK also has many strengths. It is a world leader in service exports,[1] with world-class universities and a research system to match.[2] Furthermore, a preoccupation with financial services can obscure wider, and faster-growing, sectors such as gaming and TV production. The UK is highly innovative in some important growth areas, with the value of the life sciences and pharmaceuticals sectors being demonstrated once again during the pandemic. It also has a degree of soft power derived from the cultural and educational exports that the widely-used English language supports.[3]

In uncertain geopolitical times, the UK's membership of NATO and its geographic location on offshore European islands afford a relatively high degree of security. Our geography may be insular, but it is not remote: our location and time zone afford a high degree of integration with the dense North Atlantic systems of trade, travel, and security, compared, for example, to Australia or New Zealand. In the context of both climate change and the steps necessary to limit it, the UK is less vulnerable than many other countries to the

1 J De Lyon et al., Enduring strengths: Analysing the UK's current and potential economic strengths, and what they mean for its economic strategy, at the start of the decisive decade, Resolution Foundation, April 2022.

2 Department for Business, Energy & Industrial Strategy, International comparison of the UK Research Base, 2019: Accompanying note, July 2019.

3 British Council, Global Perceptions Survey 2021, December 2021.

effects of global warming[4] and has relatively high meteorological potential to generate renewable electricity.[5]

But we are in a period of relative decline

Recognition of the UK's enduring, relatively privileged position should not prevent an honest assessment of where we find ourselves today, as we are well into a period of relative decline. The OECD forecasts that the UK economy will not grow at all in 2023: a worse performance than any G20 country bar Russia.[6]

While predictions of such significant future underperformance are uncertain, our recent experience of it is painfully concrete. Yes, Britain is a secure member of the family of high-income nations, but it is a long way from the top of this group and the gap has been widening. To use a football analogy, we are not yet in danger of relegation from the top division, but we are increasingly a long way from qualifying for the Champions League.

It is reasonable, albeit ambitious, to compare productivity in the UK with the US – the most productive large country in the world – along with the most productive large European economies (France and Germany). On this measure (see Figure 3) the broad picture has been of the UK converging from about two-thirds of US productivity towards about 80 per cent since 1970. The UK also made up ground with France and Germany from the early 1990s, after these countries had converged closer to US productivity levels earlier in the second half of the 20th century. But that phase of UK catch up came to an end in the mid-2000s and the UK's relative performance has been declining ever since.

4 www.gain.nd.edu/our-work/country-index, accessed 14 June 2022; D Eckstein, V Künzel & L Schäfer, Global Climate Risk Index 2021: Who suffers most from extreme weather events? Weather-related loss events in 2019 and 2000-2019, Germanwatch, January 2021.

5 Department for Business, Energy & Industrial Strategy, Energy white paper: Powering our net zero future, December 2020.

6 OECD, Economic Outlook, June 2022.

Figure 3: UK productivity has fallen further behind France, Germany, and the US since the early 2000s

Ratio of GDP per hour worked compared to the UK, current PPP

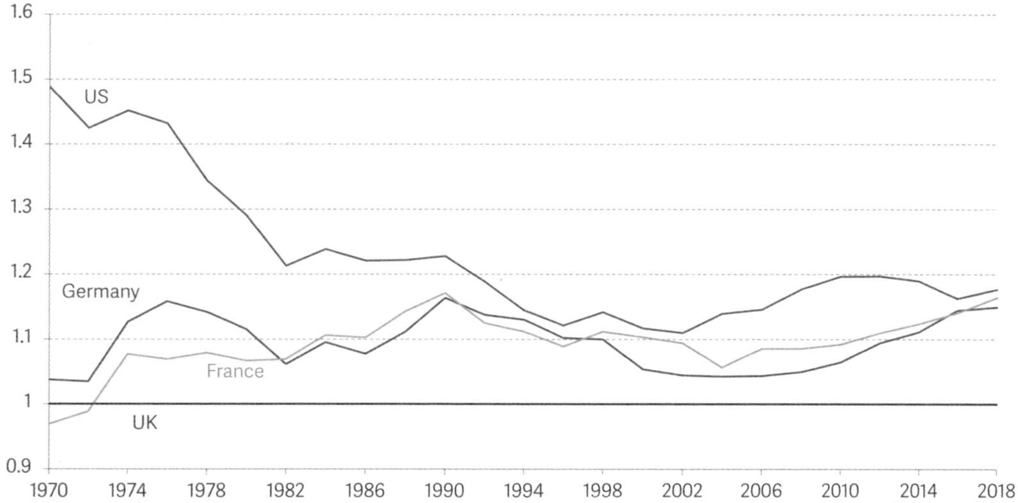

Notes: Data shown is two-year rolling averages. Purchasing power parity (PPP) is used to compare labour productivity between countries. PPP is a theoretical exchange rate in which you can buy the same amount of goods and services in every country. These data are current PPP rather than constant prices measured in a base year. Current PPP is the correct measure when comparing relative levels. See Feenstra, R et al., The Next Generation of the Penn World Table, American Economic Review, 105(10), 3150-3182, 2015.
Source: Analysis of OECD, Level of GDP per capita and productivity dataset.

While productivity growth slowed in most countries around or after the crisis, the UK's slowdown was exceptionally severe. In the 12 years following the crisis, labour productivity grew by only 0.4 per cent per year in the UK, compared to an average of 0.9 per cent among the 25 richest OECD countries (there are a number of different ways in which economic progress can be compared across countries over time, as Box 1 explores). As a result the UK's productivity gap with France, Germany and the US has widened by an average of 7 percentage points since 2008 to stand at 16 per cent in 2019. The gap relative to France and Germany has almost tripled from 6 to 16 per cent – this further decline being equivalent to an extra £3,700 in output per person.

Box 1: Comparing the drivers of living standards across countries and over time

How the UK has fared relative to some key comparator countries across aggregate measures of economic performance since 2007 is set out in Figure 4. The first segment shows the extent of the UK's underperformance in labour productivity per hour (i.e. the same measure shown in Figure 3), with the gap between the UK and other countries increasing significantly in all cases. Productivity combines with employment levels and the average numbers of hours worked in determining GDP per capita, relative changes in which are shown in the second segment of Figure 4. Here the extent of that underperformance is larger relative to Germany. On the eve of the financial crisis, GDP per capita in the UK was just 6 per cent lower than in Germany, but this gap had risen to 11 per cent by 2019.

Figure 4: The UK's relative decline since the financial crisis needs to be considered across a range of metrics

Change in the gap in labour productivity per hour and GDP per capita, and the relative change in hours worked, between the UK and selected advanced economies: 2007 to 2019

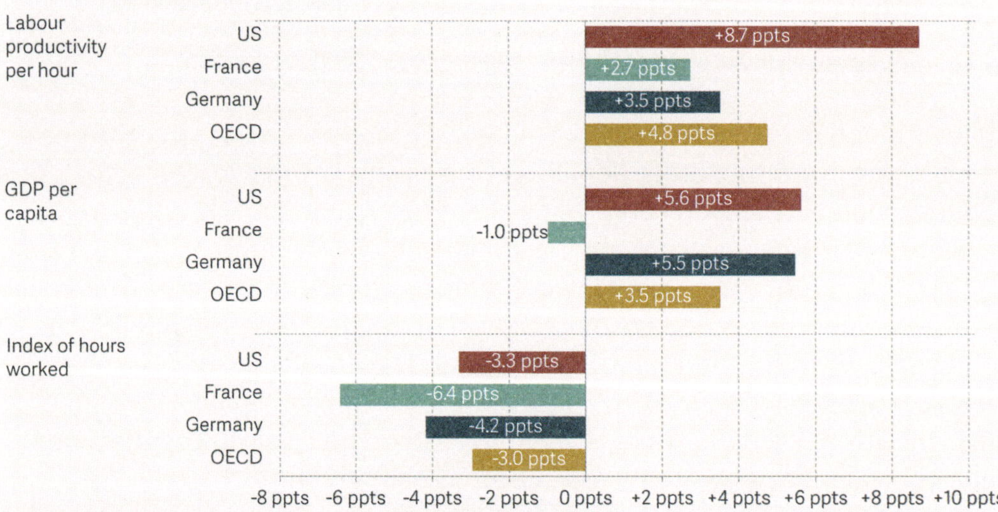

Notes: Total hours are expressed as an index = 100 in 2006. Ppts are percentage point changes. Labour productivity is measured at constant 2015 PPPs. This is the correct measure to use when analysing relative growth rates, rather than relative levels. R et al., The Next Generation of the Penn World Table, American Economic Review, 105(10), 3150-3182, 2015.
Source: Analysis of OECD, Level of GDP per capita and productivity dataset.

This difference reflects a larger rise in the total number of hours worked in the UK, which past research links to households supplying more labour to protect their incomes in the face of the deep productivity and wage stagnation in the UK.[7] Since the financial crisis, hours worked have increased by 11.3 per cent in the UK, more than two-and-a-half times the rise in France (4.3 per cent) and significantly more than the OECD as a whole (8.1 per cent).

But such large labour supply increases cannot go on forever, so provide only a temporary reprieve from the effect on household income growth of relative underperformance on productivity. In the long run it is relative productivity performances that drive changes in living standards, which is why that metric is the focus in this chapter.

These productivity gaps are pervasive across different sectors of the UK economy: we are not less productive simply because we have too little manufacturing or too many restaurants.[8] Among other things, British firms – and therefore British workers – have too little capital to work with, explaining almost all of our productivity gap with France. In the 40 years to 2019, total fixed investment in the UK averaged 19 per cent of GDP, the lowest in the G7 and some 4 percentage points below the G7 average of 23 per cent.[9] Business capital investment in the UK as a proportion of GDP (at 10 per cent in 2019) has consistently lagged behind France, Germany, and the US (13 per cent, on average), as has business investment in research and development (1.2 per cent versus an average of 2 per cent across these three countries in 2019).

In contrast to our firms' lack of capital, the UK scores well on some aggregate measures of human capital, relative both to the past and to some other countries.[10] But there remain major shortcomings and inequalities in skills (see Box 2).

---

7 T Bell & L Gardiner, Feel poor, work more: Explaining the UK's record employment, Resolution Foundation, November 2019. See also J P Pessoa & J Van Reenen, The UK Productivity and Jobs Puzzle: Does the Answer Lie in Wage Flexibility?, Economic Journal, 124: pages 433-452, 2014.

8 J Oliveira-Cunha et al., Business time: How ready are UK firms for the decisive decade?, Resolution Foundation, May 2021.

9 Source: analysis of OECD data. This is calculated as simple averages of the ratio of total gross fixed capital formation (GFCF) to GDP, in current prices.

10 B Égert, C de La Maisonneuve & D Turner, A new macroeconomic measure of human capital exploiting PISA and PIAAC: Linking education policies to productivity, OECD Economics Department Working Papers No. 1709, April 2022.

Box 2: Human capital in the UK

Significant gains in educational attainment over recent decades mean that whereas in 1996 roughly half of young men, and significantly more than half of young women, would enter their mid-20s with at most GCSE-equivalent qualifications, fewer than one-in-three do today (Figure 5). The proportion of young women with a degree has more than doubled over this period. But the pace of improvement has slowed – during the late 1990s, the average annual increase in the proportion of 25-34-year-olds with degrees was 7 per cent, but by 2017-2019 this had fallen to 3 per cent.[11]

Figure 5: The proportion of younger men and women with lower-level qualifications has roughly halved since the mid-1990s

Highest qualification held among 25-34-year-olds: UK

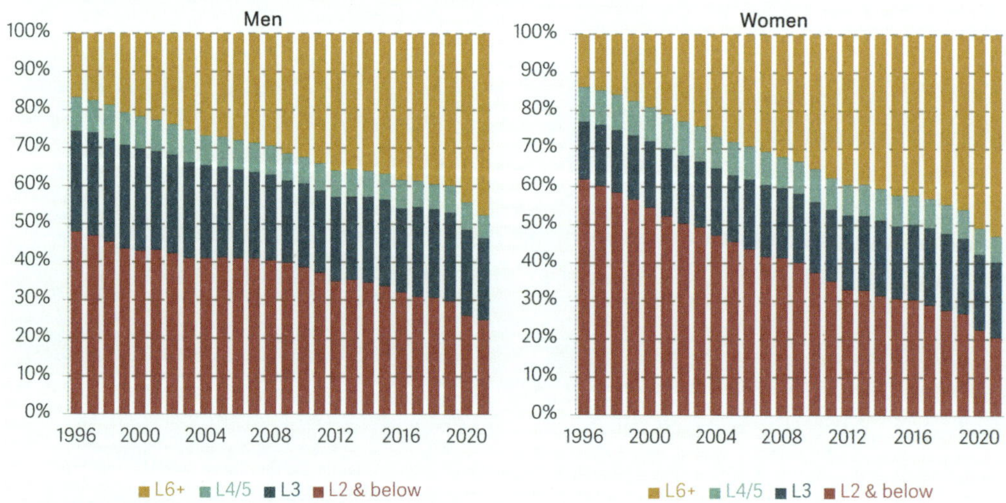

Notes: Below Level 2 includes qualifications classed as 'other' in the ONS Labour Force Survey. Level 2 is equivalent to GCSE-level qualifications, Level 3 is equivalent to A-level, Level 4/5 refer to sub-degree higher education courses, and Level 6+ refers to degree-equivalent qualifications and higher.
Source: Analysis of ONS, Labour Force Survey.

The distribution of human capital in the UK is highly unequal, with our school system's focus on binary English and maths exam results at 16, earlier specialisation, and a significant class gap in

11 Analysis of ONS, Labour Force Survey.

higher education (HE) participation posing major challenges.[12] Worryingly, OECD surveys show that the gap in numeracy skills between 16-20-year-olds who do not have a parent that attained an upper-secondary qualification (A-level equivalent) and those that did (approximately -60 points) is the third largest in the OECD, with England performing worse than countries including the US (-40 points) and Australia (-35 points). In 2012, England had the highest proportion of 16-19-year-olds that attained low scores in literacy in the OECD, and the second highest share (behind the US) that attained low scores in numeracy.[13]

Young people scoring low on international assessments today may also not be expected to develop skills once in work at the same rate that their predecessors have, because they increasingly work in lower-paid roles that offer less training compared to the past.[14] During 2019, just over 15 per cent of 18-34-year-old workers in elementary administrative occupations reported having received work-related training in the previous three months, compared with just over 35 per cent of workers in business and public service professional roles. In fact, training at work is something that British firms have been stepping away from: the average number of days an employee spent in training fell by 18 per cent (from 7.8 to 6.4 days) between 2011 and 2017.[15]

The causes of the UK's large and growing productivity gap with frontier economies have been much debated. But the consequences are clear.

Relative decline has been catastrophic for workers' wages and household incomes

It is common to hear claims that aggregate economic progress means little for ordinary workers. But the absence of much of it during this recent period of relative decline has been unambiguously bad news for workers. The direct

12 S Machin, S McNally & J Ruiz-Valenzuela, Entry through the narrow door: The costs of just failing high stakes exams, Journal of Public Economics, 190, October 2020.

13 M Kuczera, S Field & H Catriona Windisch, Building skills for all: A review of England, OECD, 2016.

14 For further details on the growing proportion of young people in lower-paid work, see: S Clarke & N Cominetti, Setting the record straight: How record employment changed the UK, Resolution Foundation, January 2019; K Henehan et al., An intergenerational audit for the UK 2021, Resolution Foundation, October 2021.

15 J Li, A Valero & G Ventura, Trends in job-related training and policies for building future skills into the recovery, LSE Centre for Vocational Education Research, December 2020.

effect of weak productivity growth has been stagnant real wages,[16] which are currently falling again as inflation surges. One year of slow wage growth is bad but manageable, but the duration of the current pay squeeze has made it transformational. After a decade and a half of pay stagnation, wages are now at approximately the same level as they were before the financial crisis, that comes at a cost of £9,200 per worker per year, compared to a world in which pay growth had continued its pre-financial crisis trend.[17] This is an historical aberration. Real wages almost quadrupled between 1945 and 2000, and decadal wage growth averaged 33 per cent from 1970 to 2007, before falling to below zero in the 2010s (see Figure 6).

Figure 6: Historically weak wage growth has been the defining feature of the past decade

Annualised decadal growth rates of real wages, real GDP per capita, and real disposable income per capita: GB/UK

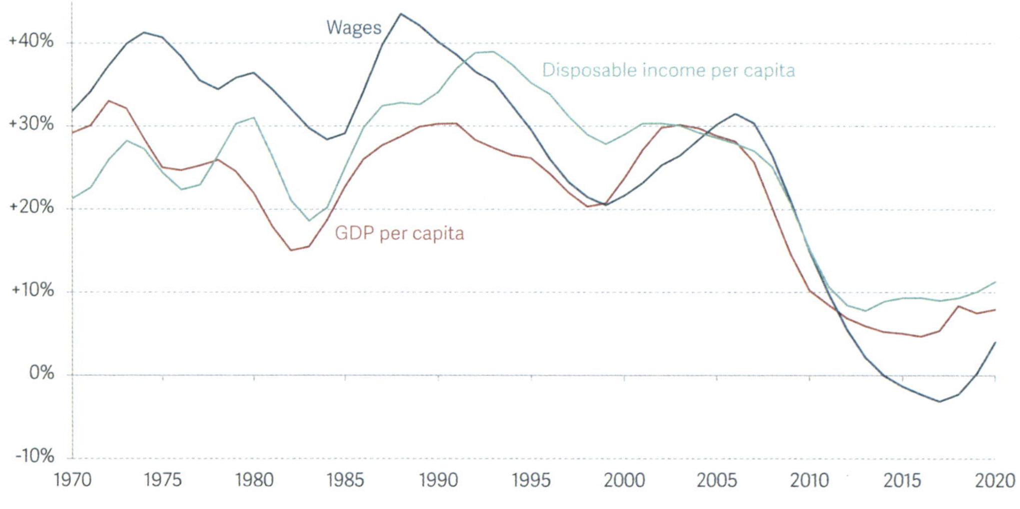

Notes: Rolling average of each variable in the three years centred on the date shown, compared to the three years centred on the date 10 years previous. For example, 2020 shows growth between 2009-2011 and 2019-2021. UK data for GDP and incomes, GB data for wages.
Source: Analysis of Bank of England, Millennium of Macroeconomic Data; OBR, Economic and Fiscal Outlook, March 2022; ONS, RHDI; ONS, UK resident population.

16 N Oulton, The Productivity-Welfare Linkage: A Decomposition, ESCoE Discussion Paper 2022-07, March 2022.

17 Analysis of ONS, Average Weekly Earnings; ONS, Consumer Prices Index including owner occupiers' housing costs.

This feeds through into real incomes, the growth of which has also slowed since the mid-2000s (albeit offset by the welcome 2010s surge in the employment rate, which rose from around 70 per cent in 2010 to over 76 per cent before the pandemic). In contrast to weak income growth, household wealth in the UK has surged, as Box 3 explores.

Box 3: Wealth, wealth gaps, and intergenerational inequality

Weak income growth is not the only trend explaining how people have experienced the economy in recent years: increasing levels of household wealth have also been crucial. Since the end of the 1980s, the total value of household wealth in Britain has consistently risen – from around three to nearly eight times GDP by the start of the pandemic.[18] The result is that while wealth inequality (which measures the share of total wealth held) has been fairly stable,[19] the absolute gaps (i.e. difference in the value of wealth held) between households has risen markedly. In 2006-08, the average wealth held by an adult in a family in the richest tenth of the population was £960,000 more than an average adult in the middle (fifth decile) of the distribution; that gap increased, in real terms, to £1.3 million by 2016-18 and is estimated to have risen further during the pandemic to £1.4 million in 2021.[20] Growing wealth, and wealth gaps, largely reflects rising values of existing assets (capital gains), rather than the creation of new ones via saving. Rising asset values have delivered huge windfalls to those with assets, while driving falls in home ownership (given the need for a deposit): 55 per cent of those born between 1956-1960 were home owners by the age of 30, compared to just 27 per cent for those born 1981-1985.[21] Meanwhile, 12 per cent of people aged 60-64 own a second home (including buy-to-let

18 K Shah, Wealth on the eve of a crisis: Exploring the UK's pre-pandemic wealth distribution, Resolution Foundation, January 2022.

19 The share of wealth held by the richest tenth of families has hovered around 50 per cent since the start of the 1980s, and the top 1 per cent have consistently owned a little under a fifth of total wealth. For more on this, and why these are likely underestimates given the coverage of the surveys used to estimate these wealth shares, see: A Advani, G Bangham & J Leslie, The UK's wealth distribution and characteristics of high-wealth households, Fiscal Studies, October 2021.

20 J Leslie & K Shah, (Wealth) gap year: The impact of the coronavirus crisis on UK household wealth, Resolution Foundation, July 2021.

21 L Judge & J Leslie, Stakes and ladders: The costs and benefits of buying a first home over the generations, Resolution Foundation, June 2021. For further discussion of intergenerational inequality and home ownership, see: J Blanden, A Eyles & S Machin, Trends in intergenerational home ownership and wealth transmission, Centre for Economic Performance Discussion Paper, April 2021.

properties).[22] Wealth gaps between regions are far larger than the gaps in pay and incomes.[23]

At a time of slow income growth it is not surprising these trends create deep dissatisfaction, as well as big winners and losers. The rising value of wealth relative to income means people are more dependent on what they inherit, rather than what they can do themselves through earning pay rises and saving: the value of inheritances is expected to double by 2040.[24] Furthermore, as wealth has become more important for people's economic lives, political incentives may shift towards protecting that wealth, risking increased polarisation across groups.[25]

These weak productivity and income outcomes reflect not just the common experience of advanced economies since the financial crisis, but the UK's relative decline. As Figure 7 shows, typical British household incomes have underperformed comparator countries and now sit below those in other North-West European countries. Whereas in 2007 typical UK incomes were higher than in each of the comparator countries shown, by 2018 they were lower.[26] Specifically, they were 16 per cent lower than in Germany and 9 per cent lower than in France.

22 Source: ONS, Wealth and Assets survey. Some of the gap between age groups will reflect life-cycle effects (e.g. older people are more likely to have been able to build up savings to purchase another property) not just cohort effects. But the wealth values of recent age cohorts have lagged behind older groups – for more see: K Henehan et al., An intergenerational audit for the UK 2021, Resolution Foundation, October 2021.

23 For further discussion of wealth and income inequality, see: R Crawford, D Innes & C O'Dea, Household Wealth in Great Britain: Distribution, Composition and Changes 2006-12, The Journal of Applied Public Economics, 37(1), March 2016.

24 J Leslie & K Shah, Intergenerational rapport fair? Intergenerational wealth transfers and the effect on UK families, Resolution Foundation, February 2022. For further discussion of the growth in inheritances and the links to inequality, see: P Bourquin, R Joyce & D Sturrock, Inheritances and inequality over the life cycle: what will they mean for younger generations?, Institute for Fiscal Studies, April 2021.

25 A J Stewart, N McCarty & J J Bryson, Polarization under rising inequality and economic decline, Science Advances, 6(50), Dec 2020.

26 The UK's comparatively poor income performance partly reflects relatively large rises in the UK price level. Over the same time period (2007 to 2018) the main UK measure of household incomes rose by 4 per cent, compared to the internationally comparable 2 per cent fall depicted here. Analysis of IFS, Living standards, poverty and inequality in the UK, median household incomes before housing costs.

Figure 7: Median household incomes in the UK are lower than in many other European countries

Median equivalised household net income: selected European countries

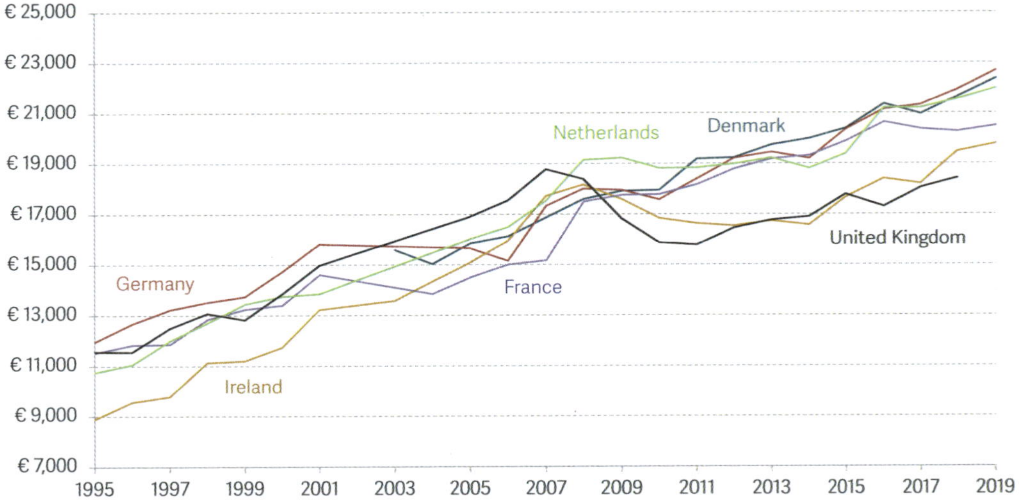

Notes: PPP adjusted. Some gaps are interpolated, including all countries in 2002 and the UK in 2003, 2004 and 2005.
Source: EU-SILC, Mean and median income by household type.

That is the toxic background to the current cost of living crisis, where double-digit inflation means real income falls this year and next on a scale only normally seen during recessions. As Figure 8 shows, non-pensioner real incomes – for rich and poor alike – are on course to be lower in 2024-25 than in 2019-20, making this the worst parliament on record for living standards.[27]

27 The March 2022 OBR forecast is based on inflation peaking at 8.7 per cent in 2022, and averaging only 2.4 per cent in 2023-24. Since then, official forecasts of inflation have increased, suggesting that a more up-to-date forecast for the current Parliament would look even worse.

Figure 8: This Parliament risks being the worst on record for real household income growth

Total real growth in median equivalised household disposable income per period for non-pensioners, after housing costs, by income vigintile: GB/UK

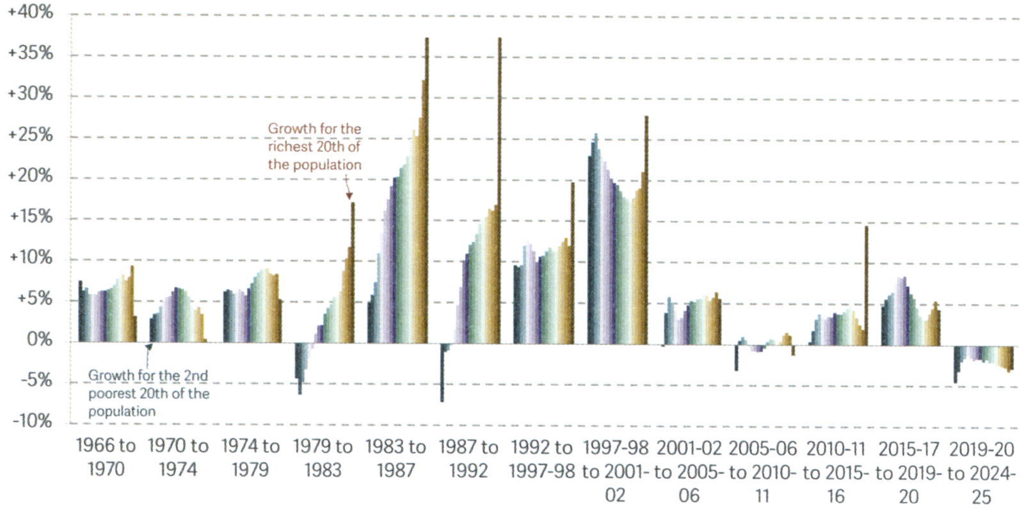

Notes: Projections as of March 2022. We exclude the bottom 5 per cent due to concerns about the reliability of data for this group. See A Corlett & L Try, The Living Standards Outlook 2022, March 2022, Resolution Foundation for details of our projection methodology. Some periods are four years long and others five years. The chosen time periods correspond to the years of past general elections (plus 2024), but we do not include a division for the 2017 election and nor do we try to estimate growth over the February to October Parliament of 1974. This analysis does not account for increases since March 2022 in both outturn and forecast inflation (pushing down on income growth) or the policies to assist households with energy costs announced in May 2022.
Source: Analysis of DWP & IFS, Households Below Average Income; and RF projection including use of the IPPR Tax Benefit Model, ONS data and OBR forecasts.

Weak income growth has been combined with persistently high inequality

Living with flatlining wages has been difficult for the past 15 years, but the UK has been living with high inequality for more than twice as long. The Gini coefficient for disposable household income increased from 0.27 to 0.37 during the 1980s and has remained roughly unchanged ever since, higher than any other major European countries but below that seen in the US (Figure 9).

Figure 9: Income inequality in the UK is higher than all other large European countries

Gini coefficient and P90/P10 income ratio for post-tax disposable income: selected OECD countries, 2018

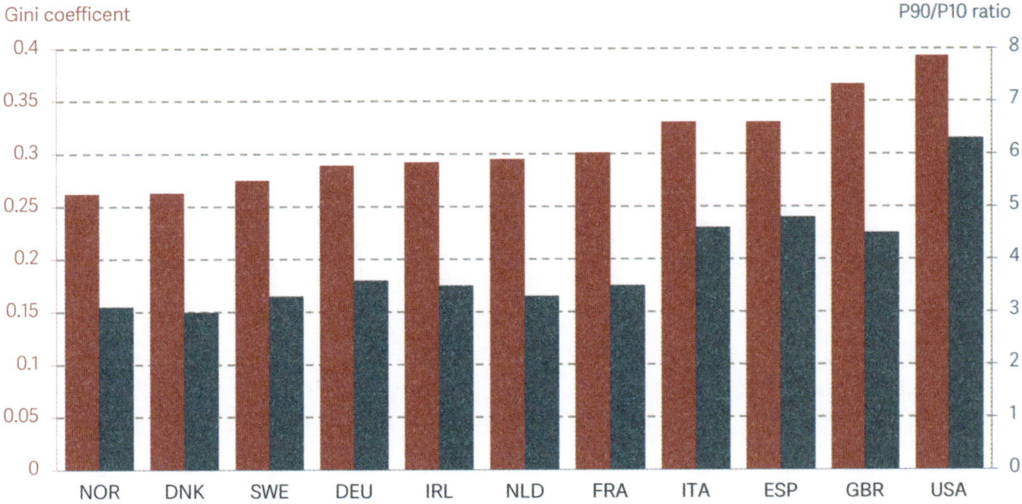

Notes: Data refers to the Gini (disposable income, post-taxes and transfers) and the P90/P10 disposable income ratio, the ratio of the upper bound value of the 90th percentile to that of the upper bound value of the 10th percentile.
Source: Analysis of OECD, Income Distribution data.

The high but stable level of income inequality measured by the Gini coefficient hides significant change.[28] Over the past two decades government policy has intentionally reduced hourly wage inequality between the bottom and the middle via the introduction and ramping up of the National Minimum Wage. Although this has taken place alongside some other aspects of low-paid work deteriorating, as discussed in Box 4, and experienced by workers in some of our focus groups.

> *"It seems to be all about how competitive we can be in this market that we're in, but they're just forgetting about the people on the ground that are actually generating this money. We just work at 150 miles an hour, and it just keeps going and going and going."*
>
> (Focus group participant, Solihull)

28 M Brewer & L Wren-Lewis, Accounting for Changes in Income Inequality: Decomposition Analyses for the UK, 1978–2008, Oxford Bulletin of Economics and Statistics, 78(3), August 2015.

Box 4: Trends in the quality of work

When viewed in conjunction with high levels of wage and income inequality, the recent relative deterioration in several aspects of lower earners' experience of work is even more concerning. Most employees are satisfied with their jobs, and there have been only limited falls in job satisfaction overall since the early 1990s among workers as a whole. But across a range of indicators – from job satisfaction, to workplace stress, to feeling used up at the end of the day – the experience of work for low earners has deteriorated: 70 per cent of the lowest earners were satisfied with their jobs in early 1990s compared to 56 per cent pre-pandemic, converging downwards towards the experience of higher earners (who consistently report the lowest level of job satisfaction).[29] Forms of job insecurity are also far more prevalent among low-paid workers and have not fallen in the way they have for higher earners.[30]

However, the rising wage floor, even when combined with recent employment growth disproportionately benefiting those on low-to-middle incomes,[31] has not translated into falling income inequality. The main drivers of relatively high and broadly stable inequality in the UK include:[32]

- While the minimum wage has reduced wage differentials between the bottom and the middle of the pay distribution since the late 1990s, gaps between the middle and top (especially among men) have continued to grow, and are now at the highest levels ever. High wage inequality is in part driven by relatively decentralised wage-setting institutions in the UK.[33]

29 K Shah & D Tomlinson, Work experiences: Changes in the subjective experience of work, Resolution Foundation, May 2021.

30 N Cominetti et al., Low Pay Britain 2022: Low pay and insecurity in the UK labour market, Resolution Foundation, May 2022.

31 S Clarke and N Cominetti, Setting the record straight: How record employment has changed the UK, Resolution Foundation, January 2019; J Cribb, R Joyce & T Wernham, Twenty-five years of income inequality in Britain: The role of wages, household earnings and redistribution, Institute for Fiscal Studies, March 2022.

32 A Corlett, F Odamtten & L Try, The Living Standards Audit 2022, Resolution Foundation, July 2022.

33 U Altunbuken et al., Power plays: The balance of employer and worker power in the UK labour market, Resolution Foundation, July 2022.

- Patterns of households formation, and labour supply choices within and between households, have been changing in a way that has further increased inequality. The UK has more two-earner and no-earner households than many other countries, while lower-earning men have reduced the number of hours they work, pushing up on inequality and making changes in weekly pay less progressive than those for hourly pay.

- While housing costs have been falling relative to incomes for the richest households since the early 1990s, they continued rising for poorer households, pushing up on inequality in incomes after housing costs.[34]

- The UK's system of pensions and social benefits reduces inequality less effectively than in many other European countries, although major differences in contributory benefits make direct comparisons difficult.[35]

Figure 10: Public concern with poverty and inequality has increased since 2010

Proportion of respondents answering "poverty/inequality" to the question: "What do you see as the most/other important issues facing Britain today?"

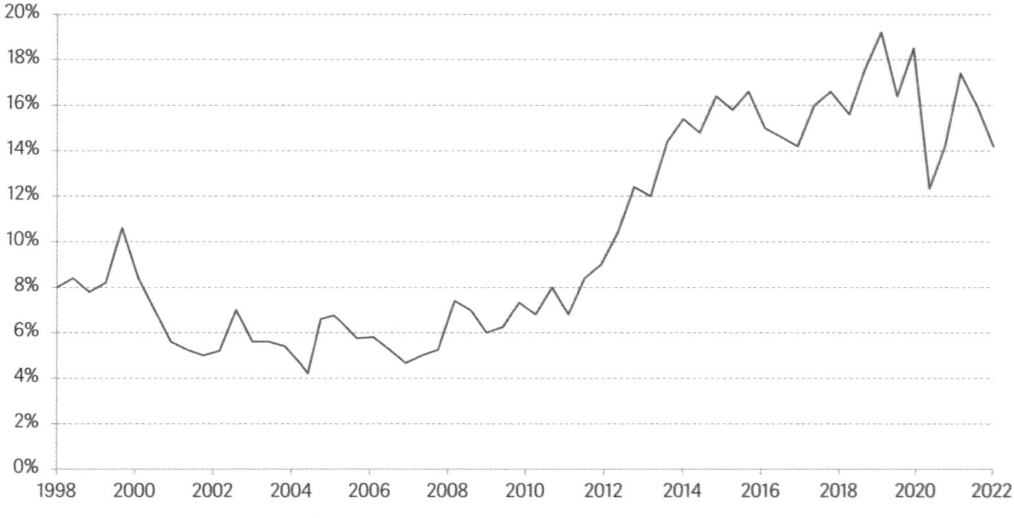

Notes: Data shown is five-month rolling averages.
Source: Ipsos Issues Index.

34 D Tomlinson, Inequality street: Housing and the 2019 general election, Resolution Foundation, November 2019.

35 Many European countries' working-age benefits and pensions depend to a greater extent than the UK's on previous earnings-related contributions. As a result, these countries' taxes and benefits appear more redistributive within any given year, relative to the UK, than they would in a dynamic or multi-year comparison.

These two features of Britain's economy – high inequality and slow growth – interact in important ways. Not least, as it appears that it is the latter feature that has raised public concern with the former, as Figure 10 shows.

It is the toxic combination of high inequality and weak growth that distinguishes the UK economy today, translating into poor outcomes for low-to-middle income Britain

The interaction of weak income growth with high inequality has much more significant implications than that on public attitudes. It means that while richer UK households have higher incomes than their equivalents in all but a few European countries, the same cannot be said of the bottom or even middle of the income distribution.

Figure 11: Rich UK households compare well to those in mainland European countries, but average and poorer ones do not

Incomes at the 10th, 50th and 90th percentiles of the household diposable income distribution in selected European countries relative to the UK: 2018

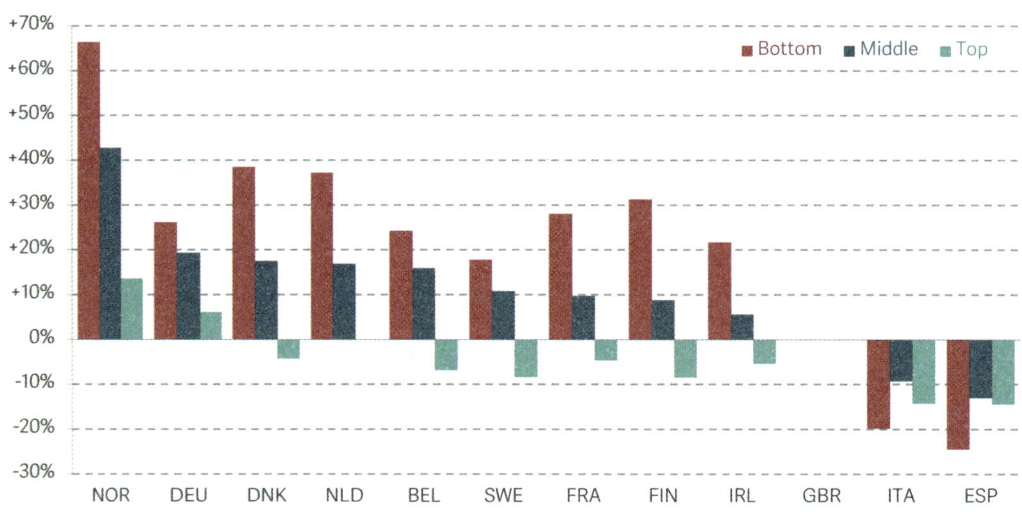

Notes: Data for the 'bottom' households is for those at the 10th percentile; data for 'middle' households is for those at the 50th percentile; and data for the 'top' households is for those at the 90th percentile.
Source: EU-SILC, Distribution of income by quantiles.

As Figure 11 shows, the 90th percentile of households in the UK have higher incomes than those in France. But, in contrast to historically similar levels, typical household incomes are now 9 per cent lower. For low-income households the combined effects of low growth and high inequality are huge: they are now 22 per cent poorer than their counterparts in France – equivalent to £3,800 a year. In fact the typical incomes of the poorest fifth of the population were almost no higher on the eve of the pandemic than they were back in 2004-05, despite GDP per person growing by 12 per cent over this period.[36]

There is nothing resilient about an economy where the poor can barely stay afloat. In the two years leading up to the pandemic, just over one-in-four (26 per cent) of all adults would not be able to manage for a month on savings alone if their income stopped; and nor would just under four-in-ten of those in the bottom two income deciles.[37] Low growth combined with high inequality means poorer households immediately struggling in the face of today's surging energy bills: as Figure 12 shows, the share of spending going on essentials among the lowest-income households had already risen from 51 per cent to almost 60 per cent between 2006 and 2019. That leaves this group little margin for adjustment and explains why price rises this year are already translating into more people seeking debt advice.[38] In our focus groups, we heard about the day-to-day struggles of living on a low income.

> *"It's impossible actually to save if on a low income...I got paid on Friday and it was gone by Monday."*
>
> (Focus group participant, Sunderland)

Of course, the impact of those relatively low incomes among poorer households in the UK are not evenly borne. Some groups are over-represented in the bottom income quartile: 39 per cent of single parents; 37 per cent of social renters; 45 per cent of adults in Bangladeshi households, and 42 per cent in Pakistani households; and 22 per cent of people with disabilities.[39]

---

36 For further discussion of international comparisons in household income levels and shares see: A Corlett, F Odamtten & L Try, The Living Standards Audit 2022, Resolution Foundation, July 2022.

37 Analysis of ONS, Wealth and Assets Survey.

38 Citizens Advice data shows a 17 per cent rise in the number of people seeking advice on debt in May 2022 compared with the previous year. Citizens Advice, Advice Trends, May 2022.

39 Analysis of DWP, Households Below Average Income, Income after housing costs in the 3 years to 2019.

Figure 12: The proportion of total spending that goes on essential items has been increasing sharply for lower-income households

Proportion of equivalised non-housing household consumption spent on 'essentials', by quintile of the working age equivalised net household income distribution: UK

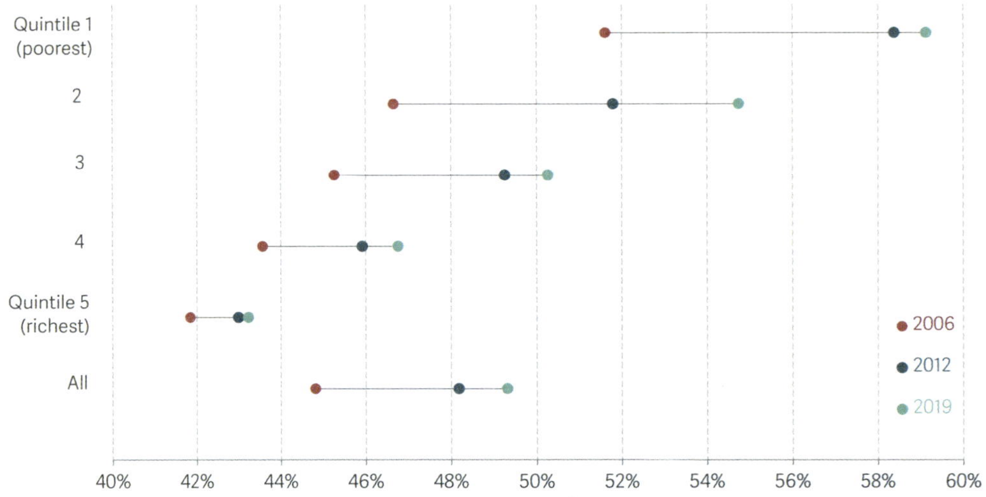

Notes: 'Essentials' covers food, fuel, clothing and transport. Distribution calculated on the basis of income after housing costs. We present trends in consumption for each individual, rather than just for the head of the household.
Source: Analysis of ONS, Living Costs and Food Survey.

It is also particularly painful for the young

The young are also hard hit by this combination of slow growth and high inequality. Slow growth necessarily puts limits on absolute income, reducing the extent to which individuals can expect to see income growth as they age.[40] This has had much more of an impact on those generations entering the labour market during this phase who would have otherwise expected to see rapid earnings growth in their 20s and 30s: the cohort born in the 1980s, for example, has experienced lower levels of earnings than the 1970s cohort at the same age. As a result, cohort-on-cohort improvements in the level of household disposable income – something that would have been taken for granted throughout the second half of the 20th century – have also slowed, or stopped, for the most recent cohorts.[41]

40 Some of this draws on: P Bourquin, M Brewer & T Wernham, Trends in income and wealth inequalities, IFS Deaton Review of Inequalities, forthcoming.

41 K Henehan et al., An intergenerational audit for the UK: 2021, Resolution Foundation, October 2021.

The amount of household wealth relative to income has grown enormously over the past 50 years (discussed above in Box 3). Britain's housing market has been at the core of the rise in net household wealth, with the growth in house prices since the mid-1990s delivering windfall gains to older cohorts but also reversing the 20th century rise in home-ownership among young adults. Today's young people are less than half as likely to own, and more than twice as likely to rent privately, as their predecessors were thirty years earlier. For example, at age 30, the home ownership rate among those born in the early 1980s was 28 per cent, closer to that experienced by their grandparents' generation born in the early 1930s (29 per cent) than their parents' generation born in the early 1950s (52 per cent)).[42] The result is that those born in the 1980s or later have borne the brunt of the UK's poor record on productivity and also missed out on the surge in the value of wealth that has principally accrued to older generations.

Furthermore, as well as being harmed by the slowdown in growth and the surge in the value of wealth, the social mobility of younger generations is also held back by high rates of inequality. There is strong international evidence that high levels of inequality also reduces relative social mobility.[43] In the UK, intergenerational social mobility was lower for the cohort born in 1970 than it was for the one born in 1958 (i.e. those born in 1970 are more affected by their parents' circumstances than those born in 1958).[44] The surge in wealth that is currently benefiting older individuals should, in time, be transferred down to today's younger cohorts, further reducing social mobility with the link between the living standards of the 1980s cohort and their parents' circumstances stronger than was the case for the 1960s cohort.[45]

---

42 K Henehan et al., An intergenerational audit for the UK: 2021, Resolution Foundation, October 2021.

43 The classic reference is: M Corak, 'Income inequality, equality of opportunity, and intergenerational mobility', Journal of Economic Perspectives, 27(3), 2013. See also: M Brewer, What Do We Know and What Should We Do about Inequality?, SAGE Publishing, 2019, for a discussion.

44 Trends in intergenerational mobility are shown in: L Elliot Major & S Machin, Social Mobility and Its Enemies, Pelican, 2018. Trends in children's outcomes as they age are shown in: C Crawford, L Macmillan & A Vignoles, 'When and why do initially high-achieving poor children fall behind?', Oxford Review of Education, 43(1), 2017. See also: S Cattan et al., Early childhood and inequalities, IFS Deaton Review of Inequalities, June 2022.

45 P Bourquin, R Joyce & D Sturrock, Inheritances and inequality over the life cycle: What will they mean for younger generations?, Institute for Fiscal Studies, April 2021.

Inequalities between places are large and persistent on multiple measures

Just as incomes are not spread evenly across people, they are not spread evenly across places either. Income per person in the richest local authority – Kensington and Chelsea (£52,500) – was 4.5 times that of the poorest – Nottingham (£11,700) – in 2019. Income from wages and salaries largely determines spatial income disparities, but the contribution of investment income to such inequality has doubled since 1997 (see Figure 13).[46]

Figure 13: Earned income largely determines spatial income disparities, but the contribution of investment income has almost doubled over time

Absolute contribution to local authority inequality (I2 measure) from different sources of income per capita (GDHI cash measure): UK

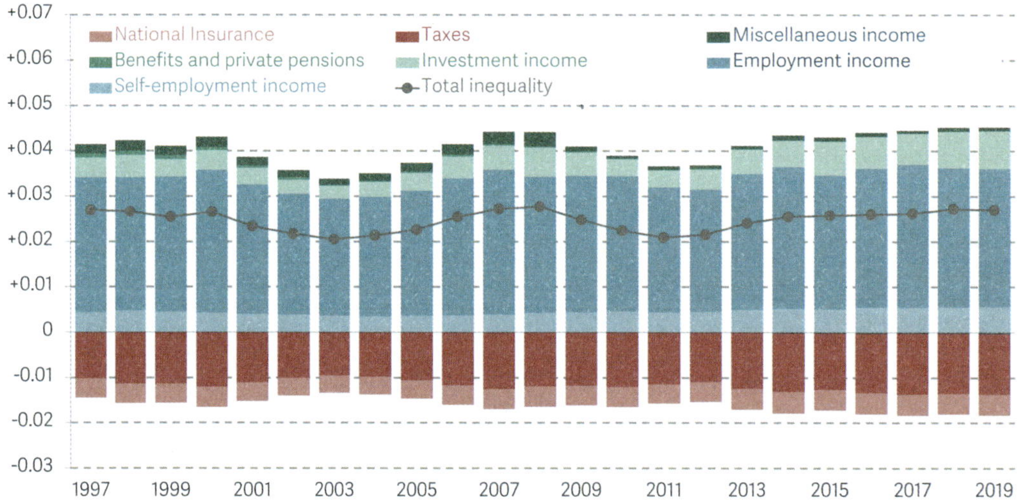

Notes: The vertical axis shows the absolute contribution to income inequality using the I2 measure.
Source: Analysis of ONS, Gross Disposable Household Income (GDHI).

46 Income here is: PAYE earnings and benefits including state pension. For more detail on income gaps between places see: L Judge & C McCurdy, Income Outcomes: Assessing income gaps between places across the UK, Resolution Foundation, June 2022.

Income from wages and salaries largely determines spatial income disparities,[47] but the contribution of investment income to such inequality has doubled since 1997 (see Figure 13). Rising inequalities in self-employment and investment income are being driven by significant income growth among those on higher incomes, particularly in London.[48] Over the past two decades, for example, average investment income per person has quintupled in Kensington and Chelsea and Westminster but only doubled for the country as a whole.

Inequalities of income and output between places are distinct, but share common features, particularly that both have been highly persistent over time. The spatial differences in incomes we observe in 1997 explain 80 per cent of the variation in the average local authority income per person in 2019. Productivity gaps across areas are significantly higher than those for income: the highest productivity place is 130 per cent more productive than the lowest compared to a 91 per cent difference for income.[49] To what extent this is exceptional internationally receives a huge amount of attention,[50] but the scale and persistence of such gaps means the case for addressing them is uncontroversial.

Productivity gaps grew with deindustrialisation in the last decades of the 20th century, and again in the first decade of the 21st as the likes of Milton Keynes and Swindon pulled ahead to become high-productivity areas (see Figure 14). As England's largest cities other than London continued to suffer from low productivity, in fact all of England's biggest cities outside the capital have productivity levels lower than the UK average. The underlying drivers of these gaps are knowledge-intensive, high productivity services thriving in larger places with access to high skilled workers, alongside large quantities of intangible and ICT capital. For example, raising the value of computer equipment per job in Manchester by 20 per cent would be expected to boost productivity by 4 per cent today, but would have made little difference in 2002.

47 We measure income inequality here using the I2 measure, which is half the squared coefficient of variation. We used the Stata package ineqfaq, which implements the method developed by: A Shorrocks, Inequality decomposition by factor components, Econometrica, 50(1), January 1982.

48 L Judge & C McCurdy, Income Outcomes: Assessing income gaps between places across the UK, Resolution Foundation, June 2022.

49 Productivity: highest, North Hampshire; lowest, Powys. Income: highest, Buckinghamshire; lowest, Nottingham.

50 The coefficient of variation between metro areas' productivity is no higher in the UK than it is in Germany. For further discussion, see: P Brandily et al., Bridging the gap: What would it take to narrow the UK's productivity disparities?, Resolution Foundation, June 2022.

Figure 14: Spatial disparities in productivity in the UK are large

Gross value added per job, by area: UK, 2019

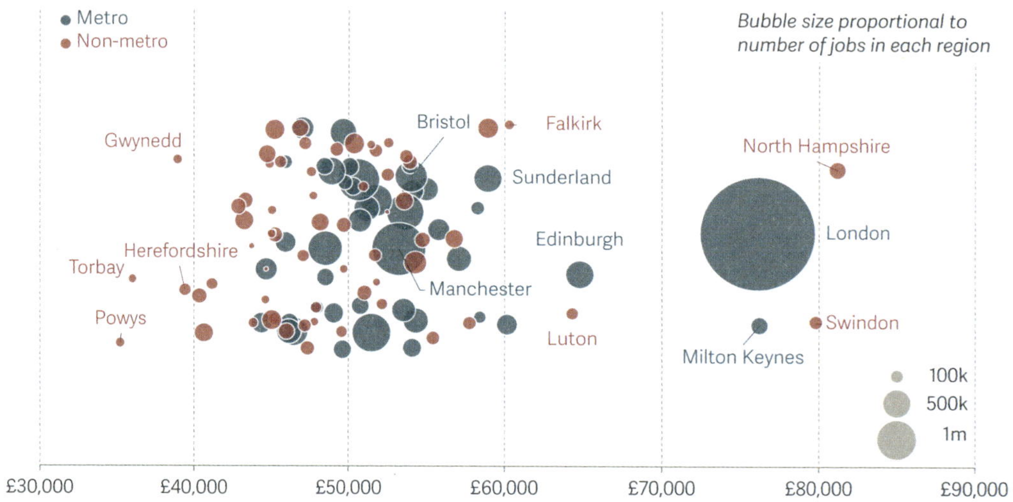

Notes: GVA per job in 2019, calculated as gross value added divided by number of jobs by workplace. Spatial units are a combination of OECD metro areas and NUTS3 for non-metro areas.
Source: Analysis of ONS, Subregional Productivity, July 2021.

Britain's low growth and high inequality equates to stagnation

The UK's combination of relative decline over the past 15 years and high inequality for the past four decades is a dangerous combination. If sustained, they risk the UK entering a prolonged period of stagnation, posing serious risks to not just our economy but to our society and democracy too.

The poor and the young are especially hard hit. Those on low incomes are left with no resilience in the face of today's fast price rises, while younger workers increasingly find themselves concentrated in lower-paying work without the compensation of benefiting from surging house prices enjoyed by older generations.

It risks public services struggling, even as the tax burden rises. Slow growth combined with cost pressures on public services mean taxes are on course to reach their highest share of GDP since 1949.[51] But despite rising taxes,

51 K Shah, J Smith & D Tomlinson, Under pressure: Managing fiscal pressures in the 2020s, Resolution Foundation, February 2022.

the quality of public service provision is continuing to deteriorate on a range metrics. The proportion of victims who were satisfied with the police fell from 74 per cent in 2012-2013 to 66 per cent in 2017-2018,[52] while the number of people waiting for consultant treatment following an referral has doubled between 2014 and 2021, from 3 million to 6 million, as shown in Figure 15.

Figure 15: NHS waiting lists have doubled since 2014

Total number of people waiting for NHS consultant treatment following referral: England

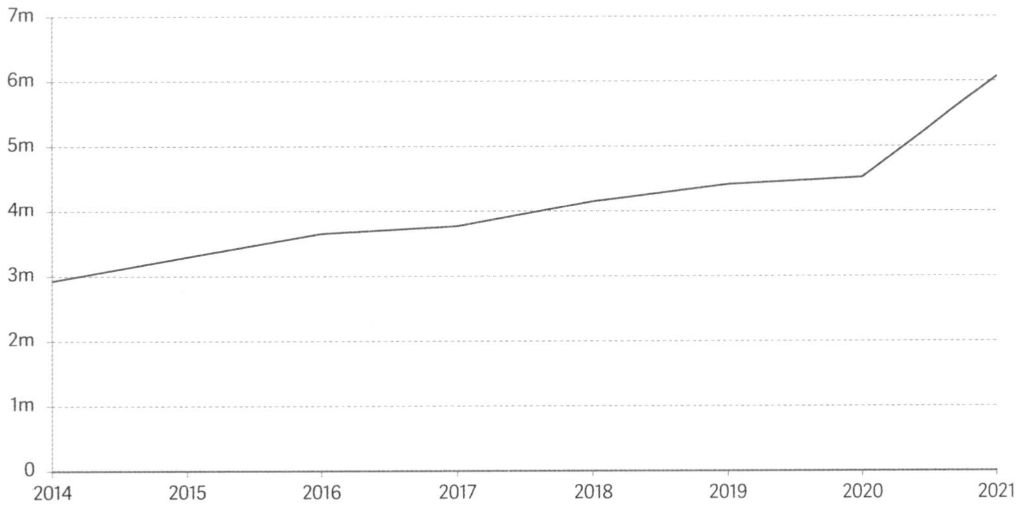

Source: NHS England and NHS Improvement, monthly RTT data collection.

The pandemic has of course added significantly to the strain on the public sector, particularly the NHS, and has demonstrated that high inequality puts further pressure on public services.[53] But even if people recognise this, the experience of stretched public services is all too common.

> *"The police just haven't got the resources to deal with somebody that's dealing drugs...But it's just not the police that don't do things. It's then the courts that don't do anything."*
>
> (Focus group participant, Barnsley)

52 Institute for Government, Performance Tracker.

53 M Suleman et al., Unequal pandemic, fairer recovery: The COVID-19 impact inquiry report, The Health Foundation, July 2021.

A stagnating nation is also less well placed to embrace change or seize new opportunities, building on the UK's science and innovation strengths. Despite popular claims that change is speeding up, structural economic change in the UK has been slowing down, with flat or falling measures of dynamism at the level of workers[54] and firms.[55] While the UK has advantages in many growing sectors, including digital technology, it is some time since those were translated into building new large companies. As Figure 16 shows, notwithstanding the importance of AstraZeneca, the UK-listed top five firms are much smaller, much older, and weighted more heavily towards banking and extraction than their US, technology focused, counterparts.[56] An economy fossilised in areas that were important for growth in periods past is not one prioritising the future.

Figure 16: The UK stock market lacks large firms in the tech sector

Market capitalisation of 5 largest listed firms: US and UK, June 2022

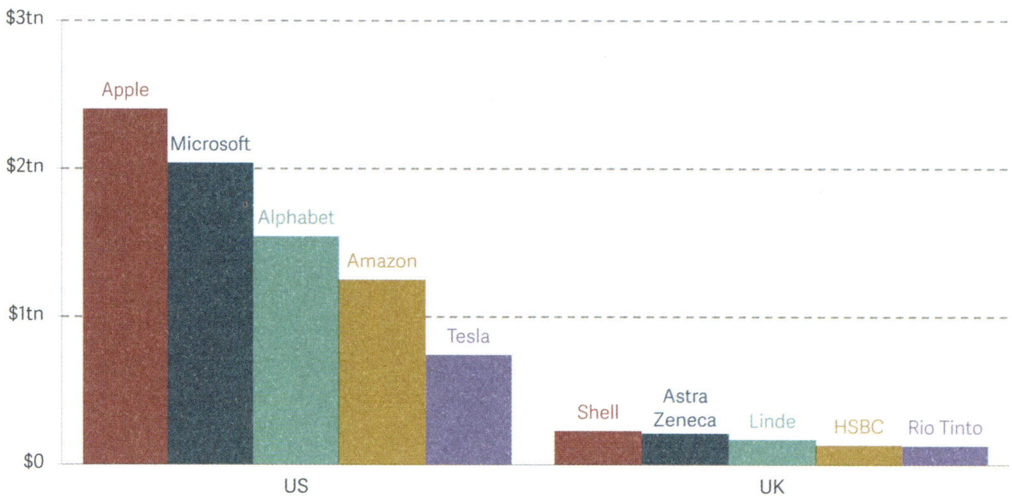

Notes: The Linde Group is listed in London but headquartered in Dublin.
Source: Analysis of June 2022 market capitalisation data, from: companiesmarketcap.com.

54 N Cominetti et al., Changing jobs?: Change in the UK labour market and the role of worker mobility, Resolution Foundation, May 2021.

55 J Oliveira-Cunha et al., Business time: How ready are UK firms for the decisive decade?, The Economy 2030 Inquiry, May 2021.

56 When interpreting this chart, it is important to note that the country a company is listed in is not necessarily where most of its value is added.

Stagnation does not just risk us failing to seize new opportunities, it also makes it harder to solve old problems. High inequality makes the zero-sum nature of politics in a low growth era even more difficult, with relative positions mattering far more. With the public prioritising lower geographical inequality, high inequality between places risks being not just economically wasteful but democratically unsustainable. Average incomes in Yorkshire and the Humber fell by 2 per cent in the 15 years to 2019; at the same time, average incomes in London rose by 7 per cent as Figure 17 shows.

Figure 17: Between 2004 and 2019, average incomes fell by 2 per cent in Yorkshire but rose by 7 per cent in London

Change in real income per capita (GDHI cash measure) between 2004-2019, and level of income per capita in 2004: UK nations and regions

Notes: CPI-adjusted, 2020 prices.
Source: Analysis of ONS, Gross Disposable Household Income.

But the experience of other countries doesn't guarantee that the pressure stagnation puts on politics will lead to its economic drivers being resolved. Educated, affluent economies can stagnate for long periods – as Italy's decline from being a GDP per capita peer of Germany in the 1980s to one of Spain today shows. The status quo being democratically unsustainable can instead lead to huge pressure on your politics, in Italy's case via oscillations between governments led by populists and unelected technocracy.

It is worth pausing on the striking fact that 25 million people in the UK weren't even born at a time when inequality was at more moderate levels, when the top 10 per cent had less than five times the income share of the bottom 10 per cent – a threshold that was crossed in 1991 after decades of remaining relatively constant at three times.[57] And 8 million younger workers – around a quarter of people in employment today – have never worked in an economy with sustained average wage rises.[58]

The UK has endured a period of relative economic decline while remaining a highly unequal country. The two combining and persisting is what economic stagnation looks like, posing dangers not only to our incomes but to the fabric of the country and its democratic institutions. As such, economic policy makers in the 2020s must tackle these twin challenges of low growth and high inequality. However, they need to do so amidst a decade of significant change, as the effects of Brexit, the legacy of Covid-19, and the net zero transition are felt across the economy. Some see these forces for change as representing partial answers to the questions posed by this chapter, while others argue that such significant disruption will pose challenges that are even more acute, so it is to the question of change during the 2020s that the next chapter turns.

57 Analysis of DWP & IFS, Households Below Average Income, based on non-pensioners only.

58 Analysis of Analysis of ONS, Labour Force Survey. 8 million of those employed in 2022 were not yet 16 in 2007.

Chapter Two

Change in the 2020s

Chapter summary

- The 2020s will be a decisive decade of change as long-standing demographic and technological shifts combine with Brexit, the aftermath of Covid-19 and the net zero transition. These will bring significant disruption for some, but not the radical reset for our economy or large job losses many predict.

- Brexit has already brought significant change – between 2019 and 2021 UK trade openness fell by 8 percentage points (four times larger than the fall experienced in France). More is to come: some sectors such as food manufacturing will grow, and others such as fishing will shrink. Rather than closing regional divides or reinvigorating manufacturing, by the end of the decade Brexit will see annual real wages £470 lower relative to if the UK was still in the EU.

- The Covid-19 pandemic saw huge shifts in how we work. Remote working, a trend which has persisted, will raise wellbeing but shouldn't be counted on to transform productivity or the economic geography of the country. There will also be less working overall: labour supply has fallen by 430,000 since the pandemic, driven by falling participation among older workers.

- Net zero brings good news for the planet and is unlikely to lead to large-scale job losses. But nor will green growth catapult Britain out of stagnation. The immediate priority for policy makers is to find a fair way to fund the investment required, particularly in home insulation: 72 per cent of low-income homeowners live in poorly insulated homes.

- There may be more job churn in the 2020s than 2010s, but the big picture is that change is slowing rather than speeding up. Between 2011 and 2021 the reallocation of labour between sectors was equivalent to 7 per cent of total employment, compared to 20 per cent experienced in the 1980s.

- Most labour market churn happens through people joining or leaving the labour force. As such demographic trends should help facilitate economic change in the 2020s as more people retire (the number of people reaching State Pension age will surpass 800,000 for the first time in 2028) and a large cohort of young people enter the labour force later in the decade.

The 2020s: a decisive decade of change

Countries can go through phases of relative stability, but the UK in the 2020s will not be one of those countries. Drivers of change shared with other advanced economies, from demographics to the net zero transition, are combining with the UK-specific shock of Brexit and a far messier recovery from Covid-19 than most anticipated.

That is the context in which the badly needed attempt to renew the country's path to economic success – including addressing the toxic combination of low growth and high inequality – must happen during the 2020s. But prevalent, and sometimes dominant, understandings of those changes – be they thinking about them through the lens of deindustrialisation or viewing either Brexit or the green transition as a silver bullet for the UK economy – do not provide a good guide for policy makers.

This chapter aims to do better, providing a study of the waves of change that have already broken over the UK economy, our judgement as to the types of impact they may bring, and a discussion of how the impact of these shocks – both positive and negative – should shape our thinking about the task facing the UK in the decade ahead.

Britain has experienced a lot of change recently

After a 15-year period of relative stability, the years since the financial crisis have been dominated by economic disruption.

A year after the vote to leave the EU, the pound settled at more than 12 per cent below its previous level, which fed through to higher inflation and a resulting increase in the cost of living equivalent to £870 per year for the average household.[1] Economic uncertainty rose and business investment stagnated.[2] But trade itself did not adjust until the UK left the single market in January 2021.

1 S Dhingra et al., The Big Brexit: An assessment of the scale of change to come from Brexit, Resolution Foundation, June 2022.

2 J De Lyon et al., Trading places: Brexit and the path to longer-term improvements in living standards, Resolution Foundation, October 2021.

As Britain was preparing for and adjusting to leaving the EU, Covid-19 hit. The downturn caused by the pandemic was unprecedented in scale (the 9 per cent GDP fall in 2020 was the worst for at least 100 years), as was the level of government support.[3] Furlough, cash for the self-employed, and increases in benefits protected household incomes on average.[4] But many people's livelihoods were disrupted, with low-paid, young, and Black, Asian, and minority ethnic workers most affected.[5] The main change for higher earners, in contrast, was home working.[6]

The pandemic also caused a very large, but predominantly temporary, shift in the composition of the UK economy, as lockdowns transformed consumption patterns: an overall real consumption decline of 21 per cent in the two quarters to Q2 2020 combined with hospitality outlays falling by over 80 per cent, while spending on food and drink rose by 7 per cent.[7] These consumption shifts have now largely unwound, but the pandemic's large and unequal impact on household balance sheets has not – the wealth gap between the richest 10 per cent of families and the median family grew by £40,000 by the summer of 2021, as richer households saved more and saw their assets grow in value.[8]

If the pandemic involved the largest volatility of output in generations, the recovery from it in 2022 is seeing the same for prices, as discussed in the Introduction. As Figure 18 shows, the period of relative stability in growth and prices from the mid-1990s to the late 2000s has been upended by the financial crisis, repeated inflation spikes in the 2010s, and incredible volatility in the early 2020s.

3 House of Commons Library, Coronavirus: Economic impact, December 2021.

4 T Bell & M Brewer, The 12-month stretch: Where the Government has delivered – and where it has failed – during the Covid-19 crisis, Resolution Foundation, March 2021.

5 M Brewer et al., Begin again? Assessing the permanent implications of Covid-19 for the UK's labour market, Resolution Foundation, November 2021.

6 J Leslie, Bouncebackability: The UK corporate sector's recovery from Covid-19, Resolution Foundation, June 2022.

7 J Leslie, Bouncebackability: The UK corporate sector's recovery from Covid-19, Resolution Foundation, June 2022.

8 J Leslie & K Shah, (Wealth) gap year: The impact of the coronavirus crisis on UK household wealth, Resolution Foundation, July 2021.

Figure 18: Sustained economic stability has given way to a period of unprecedented economic turbulence

Annual CPIH inflation and real GDP growth: UK

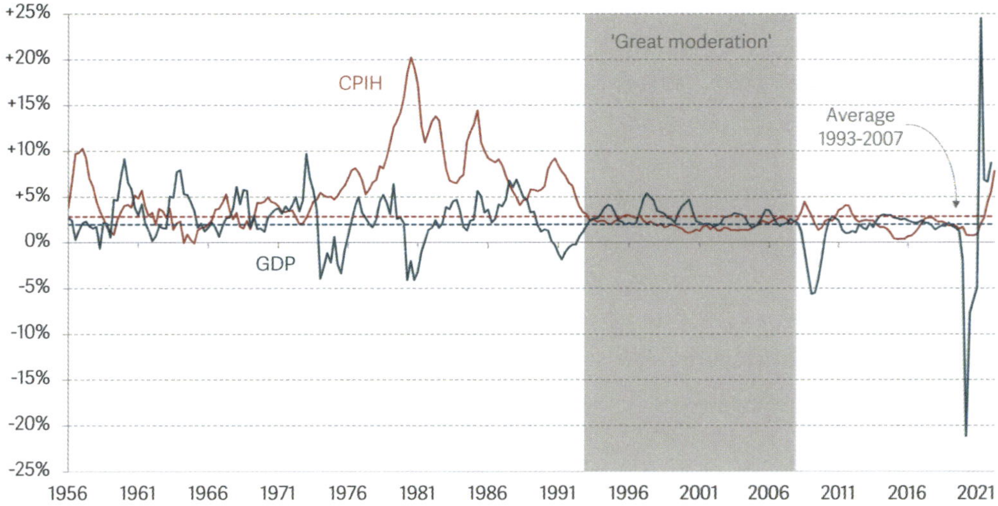

Source: Analysis of ONS, Consumer Prices; CPIH, Historical Modelled Annual Rate; National accounts.

More change is to come in the 2020s, but prominent narratives about how it will be experienced are a poor guide for policy makers

The long-term impact of the Brexit and Covid-19 shocks will unfold in the years ahead alongside the acceleration of the net zero transition. Significant change is still to come across all three areas: Britain's new trading relationship with the EU and the rest of the world, and its new migration regime, are a little over a year old; the lasting effects of the shift to hybrid working are still to play out; and the net zero transition will become much more real for workers and businesses, with large changes to transport and home heating required in the years ahead. Demographic and technological change will continue.

Understanding how these forces will affect the economy will enable policy makers to make the right decisions in managing change, and to form a clear picture as to how these changes will (and won't) reshape the context for an economic strategy.

A popular lens for considering any significant economic change is that it will be similar to the last time Britain experienced large-scale economic disruption: the deindustrialisation of the 1970s and the 1980s when the industrial mix of the British economy changed rapidly. Significant job losses, and highly geographically concentrated economic pain, followed some sectors and occupations shrinking.[9] This frame, for example, leads some people to see the net zero transition as threatening significant job losses in certain carbon-intensive industries.[10] But using this heuristic for thinking about 21st century change isn't always helpful, as the domination of largely inaccurate thinking regarding the effect of technological change in recent years teaches us (see Box 5).

Box 5: The impact of technological change on UK employment and industrial structure

The 2010s saw repeated high-profile predictions that robots would take all our jobs. Take the example of a paper from 2014, which suggested that 35 per cent of UK jobs were at risk of automation by 2034.[11] This striking fact was picked up by Monetary Policy Committee members, politicians, and researchers alike and led to a flurry of interest in the economic and political implications of the risk of elevated automation-driven unemployment, with headlines such as the following becoming a regular feature in the news: "Robots have taken more than 60,000 jobs from British workers – with 15 MILLION more to go".[12] But mass unemployment has not yet come to pass. We are now almost half-way through this period in which more than a third of jobs were predicted to vanish, and yet the employment structure of the UK economy is broadly unchanged compared to 2014.

Of course, in a similar way to other developed economies, the UK's labour market has experienced the effects of technological change over recent decades. Occupations that are more exposed to

9 J Muellbauer & D Soskice, Chapter in Economy 2030 Inquiry international case studies book, Resolution Foundation, forthcoming.

10 M Dathan, Staggering ten million jobs at in red wall seats at risk due to Government's carbon-neutral pledge, research reveals, The Sun, January 2021; T Helm, 660,000 jobs at risk as UK's green investment lags, The Observer, September 2021.

11 Deloitte, Agiletown: The relentless march of technology and London's response, November 2014.

12 M Waghorn, Robots have taken more than 60,000 jobs from British workers – with 15 MILLION more to go, The Mirror, April 2018.

technological advancements, such as machine operators and retail cashiers, have seen slower employment growth.[13] The effect on wages is less clear, with some negative impact from robotic advancements but no negative wage relationship connected to software exposure.[14]

But these correlations do not fully quantify the aggregate labour market effects resulting from these technologies, because indirect effects (including from higher productivity) are also important. For example, in recent years there has been a negative direct effect of new robotic technologies on manufacturing employment, and an offsetting positive indirect effect on services employment across local labour markets. Taken together, the adoption of automated robots has seen no significant changes in employment across local labour markets between 1995 and 2019.

Rather than starting with the default assumption that change always manifests as major reductions in employment, a better approach is to interrogate the changes that are coming and build an accurate picture of their implications. This is what we now turn to, evaluating how Brexit, Covid-19, and net zero will continue to reshape the British economy in the 2020s. Overall, we find that these changes will involve significant disruption to some sectors and the people who work there. But from the perspective of the economy as a whole they are unlikely to lead to widespread job losses, with more diffuse changes to wages or the tasks jobs involve being more likely. As such, huge labour market disruptions are unlikely to provide an alternative focus for policy makers to the high-inequality and low-growth stagnation covered in the previous chapter. Indeed, we find that the main impact of these changes may be to reinforce the risk of stagnation and the case for focusing on tackling it.

13 R Costa & Y Yu, Adopt, adapt and improve: A brief look at the interplay between labour markets and technological change in the UK, Resolution Foundation, forthcoming; OECD, What happened to jobs at high risk of automation?, January 2021.

14 For further discussion of wage polarisation, see: M Goos & A Manning, Lousy and lovely jobs: The rising polarization of work in Britain, The Review of Economics and Statistics, 89(1), February 2007; D Oesch, Occupational Change in Europe: How Technology and Education Transform the Job Structure, Oxford University Press, 2013; A Salvatori, The anatomy of job polarisation in the UK, Journal for Labour Market Research, 52(1), July 2018.

Brexit is having significant effects on the UK economy, albeit not always the ones expected

The UK is only 18 months into a new economic era, defined by accepting higher trade frictions with the EU (equivalent to a 13 and 21 per cent increase in tariffs for our manufacturing and service sector respectively[15]), in exchange for more freedom over domestic regulation and wider trade policy. The trade shock is similar in scale to the tariffs implemented during the China–US trade war, but covering a much larger proportion of UK trade and including services.

Some immediate changes following the January 2021 introduction of the Trade and Co-operation Agreement (TCA) are beginning to emerge in the economic data, albeit with uncertainty given the confounding effect of the pandemic. It is not clear whether the UK has seen the large immediate relative decline in its exports to the EU that many predicted,[16] although UK imports from the EU have fallen more swiftly than those from the rest of the world (the proportion of UK goods imports sourced from the EU fell to 48 per cent in 2021 from 55 per cent in 2019).

Instead, the impact of Brexit appears to be a more general reduction in openness and competitiveness, manifested across our trading relationships: Britain is the only large European country to have experienced a decline in trade openness in 2021 as global trade rebounded. Between 2019 and 2021, this left the UK with a fall of 8 percentage points in total trade as a proportion of GDP, compared to a 2 percentage point fall in France with its similar trade profile. The UK also lost market share across three of its largest non-EU goods import markets in 2021: the US, Canada, and Japan. The declines in Britain's share of these markets is not explained by changes in the composition of global trade during the pandemic, suggesting that a wider competitiveness problem may be emerging in the UK.

The coincidence of the pandemic with the UK's new trading relationship means that precisely isolating Brexit's immediate impact is difficult. But given that it should take several years for capital and labour to adjust to a

15 Unless otherwise stated the analysis in this section is drawn from S Dhingra et al., The Big Brexit: An assessment of the scale of change to come from Brexit, Resolution Foundation, June 2022.

16 UK trade statistics do not show a faster decline in exports to the EU relative to those for the rest of the world, but there is some tension with EU statistics, which show the UK's share of EU imports (excluding minerals and fuels) falling by 26 per cent in 2021. This is over three times the decline observed with the US, Japan, or Australia, our other large trading partners.

new regime anyway, LSE and Resolution Foundation modelling helps us to anticipate those changes that may materialise over time.

Behind a generalised fall in openness (by 2030 we expect UK firms to export 24 per cent less than if we had remained within the EU) are very significantly larger changes for some sectors (agricultural exports are expected to fall by over 80 per cent in total and by over 90 per cent to the EU) as Figure 19 shows.[17]

Figure 19: With very few exceptions, imports and exports are set to decline across the whole economy as a result of the UK's exit from the EU

Percentage change in UK exports and imports, relative to remaining in the EU: 2030

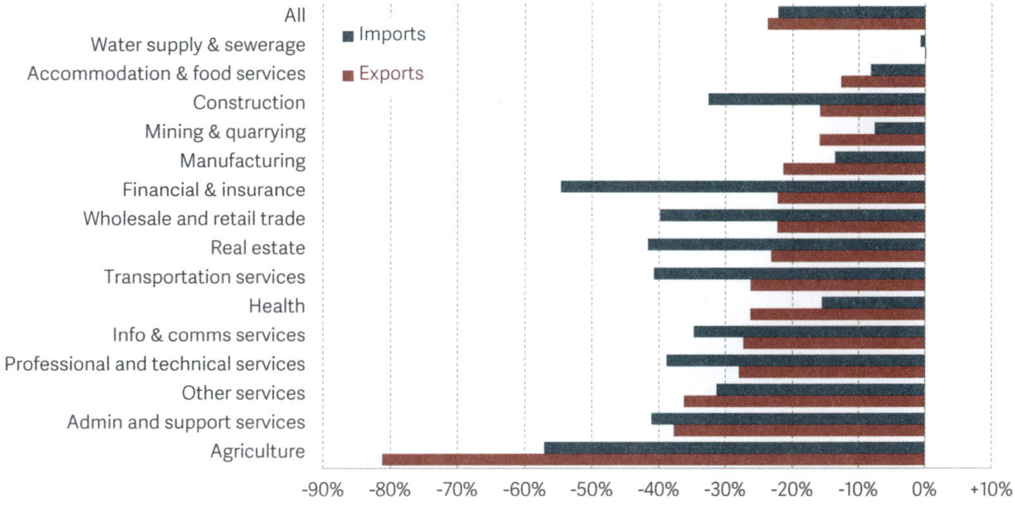

Source: Analysis uses CEP trade model from S Dhingra et al., The costs and benefits of leaving the EU: Trade effects, Economic Policy 32(92), October 2017, with regionalised inputs from EUREGIO Regionalised Input Output Database and a dynamic adjustment using ONS, Labour Force Survey.

Changes in trade will translate into big winners and losers within and between sectors when it comes to output. Within the manufacturing sector, there is considerable variation in the performance of individual industries, reflecting the differing opportunities available to them to reorient to the domestic market. A few will gain, such as food manufacturing, which is expected to be 5 per cent larger, but others will see significant falls in output, such as

17 14 per cent of this is due to the immediate new barriers introduced with the EU, and a further 9 per cent coming from forgone future EU integration.

the manufacture of basic metals. Among the primary sectors, the new trade barriers (considered in isolation) are expected to deliver gains for British agriculture, but fishing is expected to be one of the hardest-hit sectors, with output set to be 30 per cent lower. This is because British fishers are reliant on exporting to the EU for their revenues, and now face new barriers to sell to EU consumers. On the other hand, British farmers are set to benefit from less fierce import competition from EU producers, who had been successful in supplying produce to the UK market, and these greater domestic opportunities are expected to outweigh any lost market share overseas.

However, the extent to which British farmers and food manufacturers can take advantage of these opportunities will also depend on policy choices beyond trade, including on migration. Following Brexit, immigration levels are expected to be lower, and the migrants that come to the UK to be more qualified on average than they were before the EU referendum. For some firms and sectors with high staff turnover that are reliant on lower-paid EU migrants, such as food manufacturing, these restrictions will make it harder for output to grow as expected. These pressures are already becoming apparent, with sectors such as food and accommodation, which rely on EU workers in Skilled Worker visa-ineligible roles for 10 per cent of their workforce, having seen vacancies double as the economy reopened post-pandemic. While automation can relieve some of these pressures, it is not possible in certain sectors, including for many agricultural picking roles.[18]

Reductions in output driven by Brexit will mean significant labour market adjustment for the relatively small numbers of workers in the worst-hit sectors. For example, the 5,000 people employed in the fishing sector in 2019 and the 75,000 employed in the manufacture of basic metals may face a painful adjustment, with increased job uncertainty and potentially big hits to their livelihoods.[19] These changes will be significant for the workers affected as well as the places where these industries are concentrated. If they lead to involuntary unemployment, history tells us that this can do lasting damage: a long spell out of work followed by a return to work in a lower-paid role is more common for those who leave work involuntarily than those who do not, while

18 K Henehan, If fewer workers migrate to Britain, our own will need greater mobility: Migration policy can complement an economic strategy, but it can't stand in for one, Resolution Foundation, February 2022.

19 S Dhingra et al., The Big Brexit: An assessment of the scale of change to come from Brexit, Resolution Foundation, June 2022.

over the past few decades typical annual real hourly pay fell 1.1 per cent among those who had experienced an involuntary period out of work within the past year, compared to 2.1 per cent growth among all workers.[20]

However, for the economy as a whole, we expect this increase in labour market churn to be small compared to that seen in previous decades. Our projection is that additional outflows from a given region and sector due to Brexit could equate to less than 0.5 per cent of the workforce or 132,000 workers, and this will be spread over many years as the adjustment takes place not overnight but via firms' entry, exit, and investment decisions.[21]

Indeed, the big-picture structure of the economy will remain relatively stable, with the main effect of significantly higher trade barriers being to reduce our incomes relative to what they would otherwise have been. The direct impact of the new trade regime alone is that long-run labour productivity will be 1.3 per cent lower than it would otherwise have been. The estimated impact on living standards is larger, with real wages 1.8 per cent lower, a loss of £470 per worker per year relative to staying in the EU. Above average wage falls are expected in London, Wales, and the North East, which could see real wage falls of £710, £550, and £510 respectively compared with a no Brexit scenario. Meanwhile, Northern Ireland's relative insulation from some of these changes means a smaller downward pressure on wages of just 0.8 per cent or £230 per person per year. In real wage terms, finance and insurance experiences the most significant wage falls (£1,260 per person per year), with manufacturing also falling by more than the UK average (£650 per person per year) relative to staying in the EU.[22]

These estimates focus solely on the direct effect of the change in the trade relationship with the EU. The OBR takes account of wider impacts of the UK's exit from the EU such as lower investment and migration in its judgement that "the increase in non-tariff barriers on UK-EU trade acts as an additional impediment to the exploitation of comparative advantage" to such an extent that the UK's long-run GDP will be 4 per cent lower than if we had not left the

---

20 N Cominetti et al., Changing jobs? Change in the UK labour market and the role of worker mobility, Resolution Foundation, January 2022.

21 S Dhingra et al., The Big Brexit: An assessment of the scale of change to come from Brexit, Resolution Foundation, June 2022.

22 S Dhingra et al., The Big Brexit: An assessment of the scale of change to come from Brexit, Resolution Foundation, June 2022.

EU.[23] The OBR estimated that by January 2021 two-fifths of this hit had already taken place due to the slowdown in investment following the Brexit referendum.[24]

Covid-19 remains with us, but its economic effects have faded significantly

Further waves of Covid-19 look set to be regular features of the 2020s, but the pandemic's long-term economic impacts are set to be smaller and more diffuse than may have been expected when Britain was in the midst of mass shutdowns of swathes of the economy in 2020 and 2021. Young workers and lower earners bore the brunt of the impact of those changes because they disproportionately worked in the hardest-hit sectors. But, as discussed above, major changes to consumption patterns have now materially unwound, with transport being the only sector of the economy operating notably below its pre-pandemic level in the early part of 2022. This partly results from the rise of working from home (which we turn to in more detail later in this chapter) and partly reflects the slow recovery in aviation.[25] But even that recovery has now gained pace, with supply struggling to keep up with fast-rebounding demand for air travel.

More broadly, it seems that many, even if not quite all, of the pandemic changes we witnessed are unwinding. The example of retail sales is illustrative here: online sales as a proportion of total sales surged from 20 per cent pre-pandemic to 38 per cent in February 2021, prompting talk of an online shopping revolution. But, as shown in Figure 20, they have since fallen back to 27 per cent, just 4 percentage points higher than would have been implied by a steady continuation of the pre-pandemic trend.[26] This persistence is largely a result of the increase in online food shopping that has unwound only slightly since early-2020.

23 Office for Budget Responsibility, Brexit analysis, 26 May 2022. Accessed: 5 June 2022.

24 Office for Budget Responsibility, Impact of the Brexit trade agreement on our economy forecast, March 2021.

25 Aviation passenger numbers were still 42 per cent lower than pre-pandemic in Q1 2022. UK Civil Aviation Authority, 2022 quarter one flight data, 24 May 2022.

26 Updated analysis originally from: J Leslie, Bouncebackability: The UK corporate sector's recovery from Covid-19, Resolution Foundation, June 2022.

Figure 20: While most internet sales are now only slightly above the pre-pandemic trend, online food sales remain high

Share of retail sales made online, outturn and pre-pandemic trend, all (excluding fuel) and food: GB

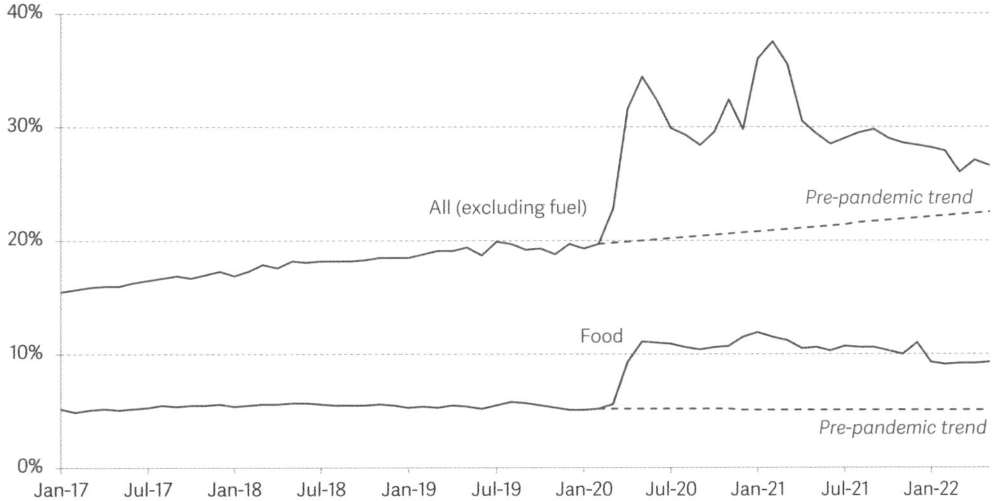

Source: ONS, Retail Sales.

It is a similar story when we look at the labour market impacts of the pandemic across local authority areas. These were initially highly uneven, with places that were used to importing spending power from tourists, students, or commuters hardest hit. A swifter than expected recovery saw many of those areas bounce back. By February 2022, most parts of the country had more employee jobs than pre-pandemic, with only outer London boroughs and places near airports continuing to be affected, and even these falls were relatively small in nature.[27] Take Crawley, the home of Gatwick airport, where the number of payrolled employees fell by 4,400 between February 2020 and July 2021 and then rebounded by 1,900 in the space of seven months to February 2022.[28] This is the local authority where the number of employee jobs fell the most by February 2022 relative to pre-pandemic levels, and even here the decline in the implied employment rate was just 2.4 percentage points and is likely to have recovered further since. Although any decline in employment, particularly if persistent, is difficult for the places affected, the

27 M Brewer, J Leslie & L Try, Right where you left me? Analysis of the Covid-19 pandemic's impact on local economies in the UK, Resolution Foundation, June 2022.

28 Some of the change in payrolled employees over recent years will be a result of changes to self-employment classification. ONS, Earnings and employment from Pay As You Earn real time information, UK, 15 March 2022.

volume of change brought about by the pandemic is relatively small. Smaller than expected labour market change reflects the fact that the Government enacted a very different policy response (including the furlough scheme) to a very different crisis (with a health rather than economic cause).

There is a somewhat larger shift in employment when looking through an industry lens. Between Q4 2019 and Q4 2021, the average absolute change in the proportion of employment across industries (defined at section-level standard industry classification) was 0.2 percentage points, more than twice the change in employment shares seen between Q4 2016 and Q4 2018.[29] One key trend driving this was the increase in work in healthcare: the proportion of employment in health and social work rose from 12.4 per cent to 13.0 per cent, reflecting greater demand on healthcare providers, the test and trace programme, and vaccination scheme, alongside falls in employment elsewhere.[30] Even with this huge reorientation in economic activity, at least by recent standards, the change in employment shares across industries was less than the average seen over equivalent two-year periods throughout the 1980s.

But the pandemic does look to have had longer-lasting impacts on the economy's productive capacity. While the recovery overall has been stronger than expected, business investment has consistently underperformed expectations: GDP exceeded its pre-pandemic size early in 2022 but business investment remains more than 9 per cent lower than its pre-pandemic peak. This reflects continued and heightened economic uncertainty and longstanding structural weakness rather than any lasting direct effects of the pandemic on firms' balance sheets. While the rapid move to home working saw some new technologies being swiftly adopted, it has not stimulated wider technological adoption or led to a new wave of productivity-enhancing working practices.[31]

The pandemic's lasting impact on the labour market also poses a headwind to growth and living standards. The feared surge in unemployment never materialised. Instead, significant numbers of workers exiting the labour market has been the problem.

---

29 Analysis of ONS, Workforce Jobs.

30 Analysis of ONS, Workforce Jobs.

31 J Leslie, Bouncebackability: The UK corporate sector's recovery from Covid-19, Resolution Foundation, June 2022.

The first year of the pandemic led to a larger fall in labour market participation than has taken place in any crisis in the last four decades, and the recovery since 2020 has been slow – and slower than that seen in most other advanced economies.[32] The fall in participation is on a par with the decline experienced during the 1980s recession at this stage, but is larger than that which took place during the financial crisis, despite a much smaller fall in employment. The latest data shows that the labour supply has fallen by 430,000 since the pandemic, with older workers aged 50 and over driving the majority of this decline.[33]

There may be very good reasons why these individuals prefer to remain outside the labour market. After all, with record vacancy levels it is likely to be their choice in many cases. But a reduction in labour supply on this scale plus persistently low investment levels are headwinds to incomes in the post-pandemic years.

The net zero transition will change, rather than destroy, the jobs we do

The transition to net zero is different from the Brexit- and Covid-19-driven changes in many ways. Rather than providing a sudden shock with ongoing reverberations, this is a large, long-term, and planned shift in the way we power our economy and produce output across a range of industries. Its key feature is the requirement for a large increase in public and private sector investment (discussed below), alongside the invention and diffusion of new technologies across the economy, changing both the mix and the nature of employment in the UK.

This change does pose challenges for those working in 'brown' jobs – the occupations that are disproportionately found in emissions-intensive industries, that will require significant change during the net zero transition. Our analysis indicates that they comprise 4 per cent of UK employment (1.3 million people).[34] While much attention has focused on the idea that the transition poses existential risks to these jobs, this is only the case for a

32 M Brewer et al., Begin again? Assessing the permanent implications of Covid-19 for the UK's labour market, November 2021.

33 ONS, A01: Summary of labour market statistics, June 2022. For more detail on rising inactivity among older workers, see: B Boileau & J Cribb, The rise in economic inactivity among people in their 50s and 60s, Institute for Fiscal Studies, June 2022.

34 The analysis of green and brown jobs in this section is taken from: M Broome et al., Net zero jobs: The impact of the transition to net zero on the UK labour market, Resolution Foundation, June 2022.

small minority that directly contribute to the generation of greenhouse gas emissions: the number of coal-mining operatives, for example, is likely to continue falling from the current level of 0.01 per cent of employment (2,700 workers).

For most brown jobs, however, the net zero transition is about job change rather than job destruction. Of those working in brown jobs, 24 per cent are large goods vehicle drivers, whose jobs will not disappear even as the vehicles they use become greener. The transition is riskier for some energy-intensive industries, but the goal is for the likes of steel production to shift towards low-carbon production methods rather than shut down. Significant job change will require new tasks and very significant reskilling for some workers, including the 250,000 people working on the 'maintenance and repair of motor vehicles',[35] since electric vehicles require less maintenance overall and workers will require a very different skill set to do this maintenance.[36]

The transition is likely to pose greater labour market challenges in some other advanced economies, reflecting the fact that the UK has a smaller proportion of industrial employment than many comparators (in 2019, 18 per cent of UK employment was in industry, in contrast to 27 and 24 per cent respectively in Germany and Japan).[37]

The extent of labour market change extends beyond occupations most prevalent in emissions-intense sectors. A further 13 per cent of jobs – 'green' jobs – can be identified as those that already involve green tasks to a significant extent (and are not prevalent in emissions-intense sectors) and will be needed in order to actively support the net zero transition. This transition will mean significant changes for many workers, but this will mostly involve shifts in the tasks people undertake and the technology they use, rather than swift job losses or changes in the UK's employment structure.

Some specific green jobs (for example wind turbine engineers) are expected to grow over the 2020s and beyond, creating well-paid roles in parts of the country that are well positioned to benefit from this shift. Residents in Hull told us that they could see the expansion of the new industry (wind turbine production) happening before their eyes.

35 ONS, Business Register and Employment Survey: Table 2, November 2021.

36 The Economist, Servicing and repairing electric cars requires new skills, October 2021.

37 The World Bank, Employment in industry (% of total employment) (modelled ILO estimate).

> *"[Siemens] are continuously building. Every time you go down there it seems to have got bigger and bigger."*
>
> (Focus group participant, Hull)

So net zero has clear benefits for certain parts of the economy as well as the planet, but it also poses significant challenges for the living standards of some households, given the need to finance the scaling up of large investments during the 2020s. These challenges will largely be felt by households as consumers – of home heating or transport - and should be the focus for policy makers because handled badly they risk reinforcing the challenges of high inequalities and stagnant living standards, as well as undermining support for the net zero transition itself.

The investment costs associated with net zero are large (£1.4 trillion by 2050). While significant savings will flow from them, given the lower operating costs of low-carbon technologies (£1.1 trillion), they will materialise over a longer period of time.[38] So, while the net costs of net zero are very far from ruinous (less than 1 per cent of GDP over the next 30 years), questions about who pays for upfront investments (and how they do it) are key to protecting the living standards of poorer households and maintaining the UK's impressive consensus on climate change policy.

The 2020s will see the net zero transition moving from the backstage of decarbonising our electricity generation into the heart of the public's day-to-day lives, with emissions from surface transport and buildings needing to fall by as much as 72 per cent and 48 per cent respectively by 2035, relative to 2020 levels.[39] These changes are what is required if the UK is to follow a 'balanced' path to net zero by 2050; of course politics and economics may mean that reductions of this scale do not come to pass despite their importance.

The fast-falling costs, and rapid take-up, of electric vehicles, means that the most difficult challenge during the 2020s will be homes. Over the decade to 2031-32, this will require a capital spend of £39 billion on efficiency measures

---

38 J Marshall & A Valero, The Carbon Crunch: Turning Targets Into Delivery, Resolution Foundation, September 2021.

39 J Marshall & A Valero, The Carbon Crunch: Turning Targets Into Delivery, Resolution Foundation, September 2021.

(insulating walls and roofs) and £37 billion on clean heat,[40] with spending accelerating rapidly over the next six years to peak at £14 billion of investment in 2028 (as Figure 21 shows).[41]

Figure 21: Investment in residential buildings needs to increase drastically in the 2020s

Annual additional capital investment in residential buildings: UK

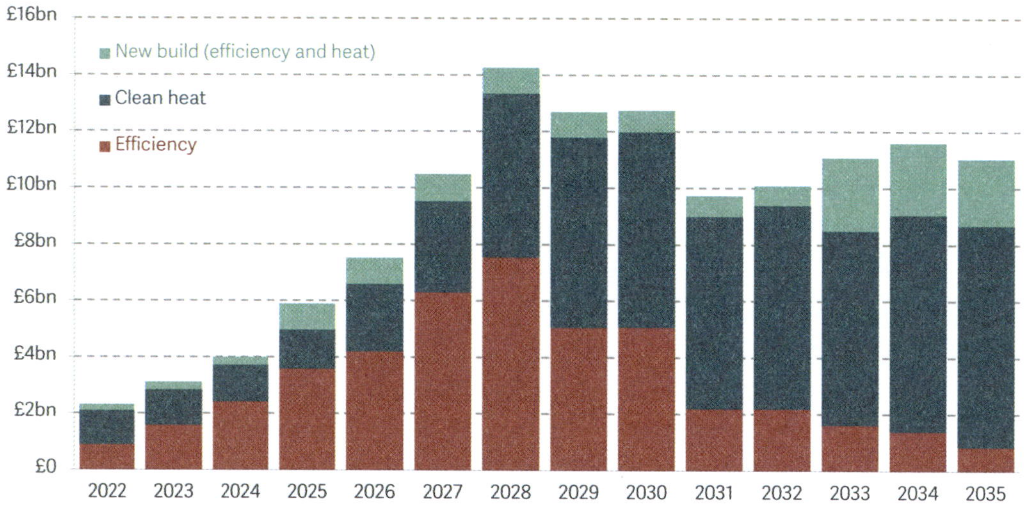

Source: Analysis of Climate Change Committee, Sixth Carbon Budget data.

These investments, and others required to deliver net zero, will come at some cost to household consumption. But whose consumption is affected, and when, is highly dependent on the different funding routes chosen, be that households self-funding, paying via levies on energy bills, or via taxation. Whether those costs are borne up front or paid tomorrow via borrowing is also important. Ensuring that costs to consumers are fairly distributed during a long-lasting squeeze on household incomes is the key to the next stage of the net zero transition. In the 2020s, this is principally about homes and their energy efficiency. There is clearly a risk of outright failure on this front, with progress having stalled after a 90 per cent fall in insulations since 2013, making the climb back up to the Government's ambition of 1 million home energy efficiency installations a year by 2030 much steeper than it otherwise would

40 Climate Change Committee, Sixth Carbon Budget, December 2020.

41 These projections are in some respects optimistic, for example in assuming that there will be no waste of capital. The actual spend in the 2020s and 2030s may be higher.

have been.[42] The biggest immediate barrier will be low-income home owners, 72 per cent of whom will need their homes' energy efficiency to be improved, but who are unsupported by government policy.[43]

Overall, change in the 2020s is likely to accelerate from recent lows and be highly disruptive for some, but we will not see a return to the rapid change of earlier decades

Together these three big, but very different, shocks and transitions mean the 2020s will bring significant changes to our economy. There will be big impacts on some firms, workers, and consumers, but for the labour market as a whole the scale of change will not be transformative, with the most significant common effect being broadly felt headwinds to already weak income growth.

We should expect more labour market churn in the rest of the 2020s than in the 2010s, with rates of both voluntary and involuntary job moves increasing. More of the former would be good news, but more involuntary job losses would entail a higher number of people experiencing both the emotional and financial hits that it involves.[44] As such, it is to be welcomed that we are unlikely to see a decade of very high restructuring of the kind most recently seen during the 1980s, instead with the change set to take place doing so over long periods of time and often altering the content of people's jobs rather than endangering them.

This also reflects the fact that, rather than speeding up as is commonly assumed, the story of Britain's labour market over the past two decades is one of declining aggregate and individual-level job changes following the rapid deindustrialisation of the 1970s and 1980s. As shown in Figure 22, between 2011 and 2021 the reallocation of labour between sectors was equivalent to 7 per cent of total employment, which was markedly lower than the 20 per cent experienced in the 1980s.[45]

---

42 See Table 10 in: Department for Business, Energy & Industrial Strategy, Net Zero Strategy: Build Back Greener, October 2021.

43 A Corlett & J Marshall, Shrinking footprints: The impacts of the net zero transition on households and consumption, Resolution Foundation, March 2022.

44 N Cominetti et al., Low Pay Britain 2022: Low pay and insecurity in the UK labour market, Resolution Foundation, May 2022.

45 The analysis in this section is from: N Cominetti et al., Changing jobs? Change in the UK labour market and the role of worker mobility, Resolution Foundation, January 2022.

Figure 22: The rate of sectoral change has fallen since the 1980s

Sectoral reallocation in the 10 years to date shown, expressed as a proportion of total employment: UK

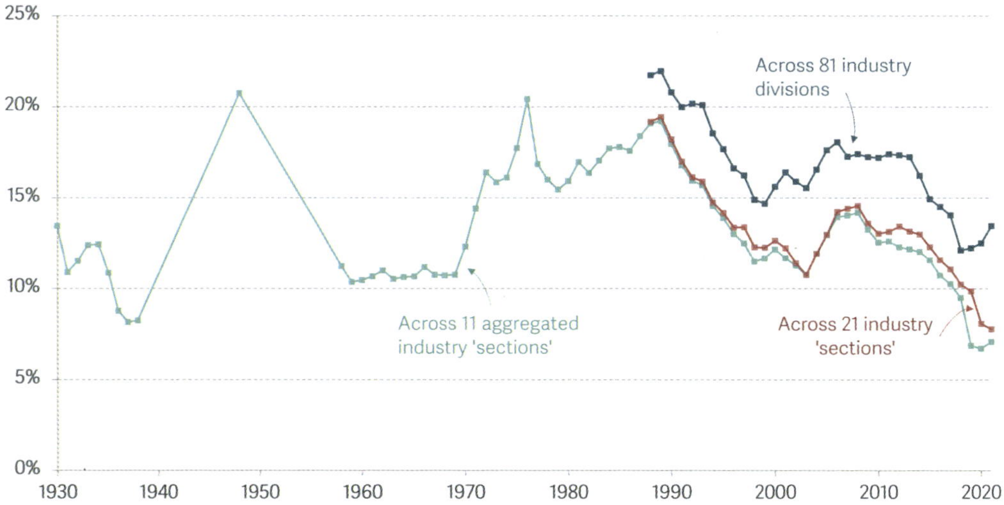

Notes: Sectoral reallocation is measured as the weighted average, across sectors, of the absolute change in employment share compared to a decade ago, based on a measure used in G Chodorow-Reich & J Wieland, Secular Labor Reallocation and Business Cycles, Journal of Political Economy 128(6), April 2020. Red line uses SIC 2007 sections but some have been condensed for consistency with long-run data; the blue line uses the full set of industry sections in SIC 2007, for which Workforce Jobs data is available from 1978 onwards.
Source: Analysis of ONS, Workforce Jobs; Bank of England, Millennium of Macroeconomic Data.

Job mobility at the individual level has also fallen this century, with the proportion of workers switching job each quarter declining by 25 per cent between 2000 and 2019, from 3.2 per cent to 2.4 per cent. While policy debates often focus on labour market change taking place through workers moving between occupations and sectors, the majority of change happens via people moving into (and out of) the labour market. As a result, demographic shifts play a key role, as well as driving economic change directly, as Box 6 discusses.

Box 6: Demographic change in the 2020s

Discussion of the economic impact of demographic change tends to focus on the important fiscal implications. However, demographic shifts have wider economic impacts that are often overlooked, such as changing the shape of the labour market and influencing the goods and services we consume.

As shown in Figure 23, between 2020 and 2030, the UK's population is expected to grow by 2.1 million (3.2 per cent). The number of people in older age (65 and above) is expected to increase by around 2.5 million (20 per cent), compared to an increase in the number of working-age people (16-64) of 760,000 (2 per cent).[46] In contrast, due to falling fertility rates, the number of people aged 15 and under is projected to decline by 1.1 million (9 per cent).

Figure 23: The UK's pensioner population will have doubled between the 1960s and 2030s, partially offset by a small increase among those of working age

Historic and projected population estimates, by age group: UK, 1961-2050

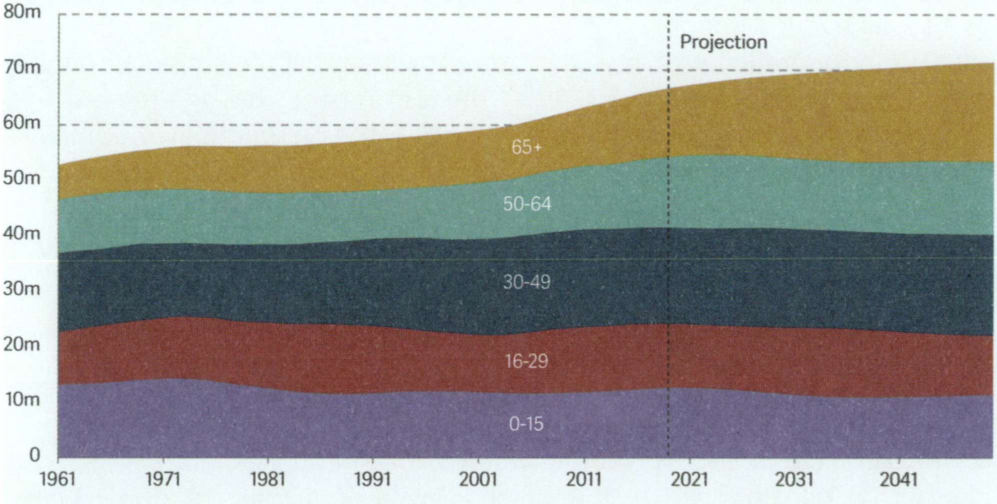

Source: ONS, Estimates of the population for the UK, England and Wales, Scotland and Northern Ireland: Mid-2020 edition, June 2021; ONS, National population projections: 2020-based, January 2022.

46 The analysis in this box is sourced from: M Broome, Big welcomes and long goodbyes: The impact of demographic change in the 2020s, Resolution Foundation, June 2022.

Over the next decade, we expect these population changes to drive economic change but also to facilitate it through a rising number of workforce exits (driven by baby boomers leaving the labour market) and entrants (driven by a wave of young people entering the labour market). For example, we find that 'life cycle' flows in and out of the labour market could reach record highs in the coming decades, with the number of people reaching state pension age expected to surpass 800,000 in 2028 for the first time ever, while the number of people turning 22 will exceed 900,000 in 2032 for the first time this century.

The large volume of life cycle-related labour market entry and exit may also offer a temporary boost to labour market mobility because, in contrast to the population as a whole, the age composition of the workforce is expected to become marginally younger by the early 2030s (the proportion of workers aged 16-29 will increase by 1 percentage point between 2019 and 2035). These effects will, however, be short lived as lifecycle flows begin to slow from the mid-2030s and the share of the UK's workforce comprised of mid- and older-aged workers begins to grow.

Demographic change will also alter the shape of the economy through adjustments in the balance, and overall level, of private expenditure. Because young people and old people spend their money in different ways, we expect age-related shifts in the population to increase the total amount of spending on recreation and culture by 4.5 per cent and private healthcare by 6.7 per cent over the next decade. While the latter is unlikely to have a dramatic effect on the shape of the UK's economy, the real impact from age-related shifts in the population will come from a huge rise in demand for – and employment of – health and social care workers predominantly funded via the public sector.

How should policy makers think about the change to come in the 2020s? Given the significant effects on some workers, for example fishers, they should recognise that 'bad change' (i.e. that which is involuntary) has not always been well managed in the past. But they should also be alive to the fact that lower rates of change in recent decades have seen some workers miss out on the gains from 'good change' as workers take up new opportunities: on average, those moving jobs enjoy typical pay growth that is 4 percentage points higher than individuals staying put. Reconciling these concerns, and the common challenge that low levels of income protection provided by our welfare state pose to both of them, is a subject we return to in Chapter Four.[47]

We should be cautious of claims that derive silver linings from change in the 2020s

While some overdo the dangers of rapid and disruptive change, there are others who celebrate the big changes of the 2020s – or parts of them – because of their perceived potential to solve major challenges facing the UK economy. These are most evident in people identifying economic silver linings to sectoral adjustments that might follow Brexit or due to changes in working practices arising from the pandemic. Such claims are overstated, and certainly not the best lens through which to understand the changes occurring in the 2020s. Some argue that meeting the UK's net zero targets provides a silver bullet for a return to strong, equitable growth, but this is unlikely to be the case.

For some, a potential benefit of the UK's exit from the EU is a partial reversal of the decline of manufacturing, with the hope that this will help narrow the UK's large regional divides. The argument rests on the idea that replacing membership of the Single Market (with its unique liberalisation of trade in services) with a free trade agreement with the EU that largely only covers goods trade relatively favours those parts of the country that are manufacturing-heavy at the expense of London and the South East.[48]

Our modelling of the lasting impact of the TCA does not support this view. While some manufacturing sectors will grow to service the domestic market (most notably food manufacturing), others (including chemicals and electronics) will shrink as we no longer play such an active role in some international supply chains, as Figure 24 shows.

47 The UK's low level of income protection is discussed in greater detail in: M Brewer et al., Social insecurity: Assessing trends in social security to prepare for the decade of change ahead, Resolution Foundation, January 2022.

48 M Sandbu, Brexit and the future of UK capitalism, The Political Quarterly, April 2019.

Figure 24: Many sectors will experience slower growth now that we've left the EU, but some low-productivity manufacturing sectors will grow at a faster pace

Long-run change in UK gross output across sectors relative to a no-Brexit baseline

Notes: Width of bars represent the size of the sector (gross output in the baseline). Static form of the model is used as it can provide a more detailed sectoral breakdown of the results. See Annex 3 sensitivities from Dhingra et al., The Big Brexit: An assessment of the scale of change to come from Brexit, Resolution Foundation, June 2022 for more information of the difference between the two models results.
Source: Analysis uses CEP trade model from S Dhingra et al., The costs and benefits of leaving the EU: trade effects, Economic Policy 32(92), October 2017 with regionalised inputs from EUREGIO Regionalised Input Output Database

The net effect is very small, and in fact amounts to around a 0.1 percentage point fall in manufacturing's proportion of gross output. More concerning, however, is that the average productivity of the parts of manufacturing that the TCA shrinks are much higher (£47 per hour) than the parts it helps to grow (£37 per hour).[49] Claims that a new migration regime, which Brexit has given the UK significantly more control over, will drive a shift towards a high-wage economy are also overdone, as are claims that lower migration will have very significant negative effects.[50]

49 Dhingra et al., The Big Brexit: An assessment of the scale of change to come from Brexit, Resolution Foundation, June 2022.

50 "We are not going back to the same old broken model with low wages low growth, low skills and low productivity all of it enabled and assisted by uncontrolled immigration." Boris Johnson, Boris Johnson's keynote speech – We're getting on with the job, Conservative Party Conference, October 2021.

Some have looked to the Covid-19-induced shift towards home working as a positive change that will be the answer to Britain's low productivity or high regional economic inequalities (suggesting it will widen the range of places in which higher-qualified and -earning professionals can live and make them more productive). The shift towards remote working is certainly significant: the proportion of people who reported that they worked from home on a regular basis increased from 5 per cent in 2010 to 10 per cent on the eve of the pandemic, but surged during the pandemic and remained elevated at 38 per cent of all workers in early 2022.[51]

However, the evidence that a significant rise in home working will raise well-being is significantly stronger than indications it will raise productivity. Of those businesses adopting home working as a permanent part of their business model, fewer than half report increased productivity as a driver, while 86 per cent of large businesses cite improved staff well-being as important.[52] Indeed, this matches evidence from workers themselves, where 53 per cent report wanting to work from home all or some of the time compared to 28 per cent who do not want to work from home. There are several potential avenues through which increased home working could increase productivity, with one of the most important being workers choosing to partially substitute commuting time for longer working hours.[53] But much of the potential benefits from home working should have already happened, as the growth in the prevalence of home working has now slowed, if not started to reverse.[54] Benefits from longer-term dynamic improvements due to, for example, better matching of workers to jobs are still speculative at this stage.

The evidence to date suggests that the impact on regional inequalities will also be limited. Hybrid, rather than fully remote, working is the new normal for professionals, which may facilitate some longer commutes within regions but not large numbers of people living in entirely different regions from their employers. There is some evidence of shifting spending power from city centres to residential high streets, but this is largely a shift that has occurred within particular conurbations or areas. The net change in work done in

51 M Brewer, J Leslie & L Try, Right where you left me? Analysis of the Covid-19 pandemic's impact on local economies in the UK, Resolution Foundation, June 2022.

52 J Leslie, Bouncebackability: The UK corporate sector's recovery from Covid-19, Resolution Foundation, June 2022.

53 N Bloom et al., Does working from home work? Evidence from a Chinese experiment, The Quarterly Journal of Economics, February 2015.

54 J Leslie, Bouncebackability: The UK corporate sector's recovery from Covid-19, Resolution Foundation, June 2022.

an area (accounting for falling office work and increased home working) is generally small and not related to the gross workplace mobility falls (see Figure 25), because areas with large falls in people travelling to the office also have big increases in residents home working. Bigger shifts are largely a phenomenon playing out between inner and outer London, with work done estimated to have increased by 20 per cent in Lewisham but to have declined by a similar amount in Westminster.

Figure 25: Work from home has caused shifts in the location of work within, rather than between, places

Estimated change in work done in local authority from pre-Covid to 2022, and change in travel to workplace from January-February 2020 to April 2022, by local authority: England and Wales

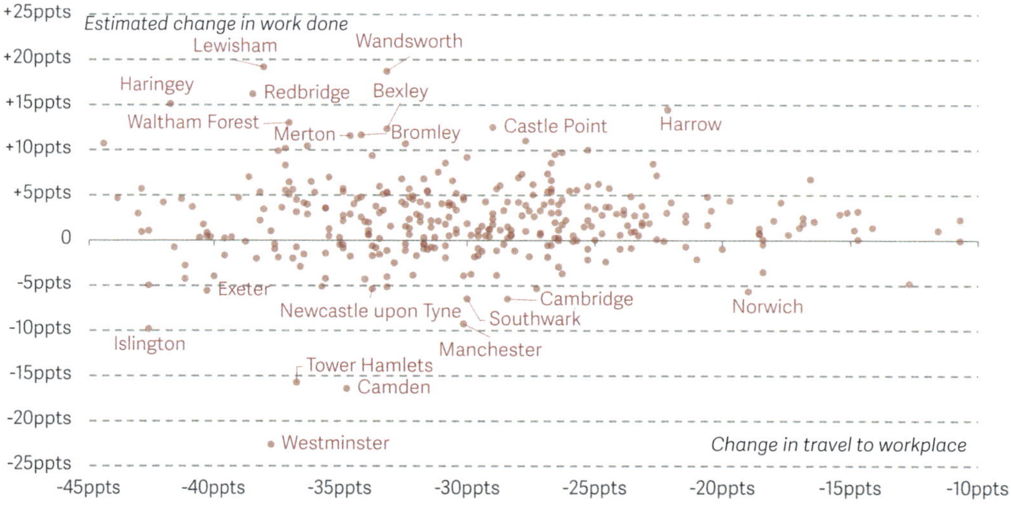

Source: Google mobility data; De Fraja et al., Covid reallocation of spending: The effect of remote working on the retail and hospitality sector, SERPS no. 2021006, December 2021.

Even when home working has meant a big shift towards more work being done in a local authority, it does not appear to have helped the lower earners living there. Haringey is a striking example, combining a big rise in working from home with a larger rise in the claimant count than anywhere bar Newham.[55]

Working from home will bring benefits to people (raising well-being even if not productivity) and some places (a 5 per cent increase in work done in Wigan has a material impact). But overall, it looks like a significant silver lining related to

55 M Brewer et al., Right where you left me? Analysis of the Covid-19 pandemic's impact on local economies in the UK, Resolution Foundation, June 2022.

hybrid working, which transforms the UK's economic outlook or geography, has not materialised.

Claims of pandemic induced productivity gains also need to be tempered by recognising its wider effects. For example, a drag on longer term productivity could come thanks to school closures and disruptions leading to, highly unequal, learning losses for children: during the autumn of 2020, local authorities with the highest proportions of pupils receiving free school means (FSM) experienced nine-and-a-half days of lost learning per pupil, while local authorities with the lowest proportion of students receiving FSM experienced two lost days.[56]

Green growth is desirable but not a silver bullet for the UK's structural challenges

For some, the net zero transition offers much more than a silver lining, being seen as a silver bullet for economies, like the UK's, struggling with slow growth. On this view, net zero is more than simply the route to reducing the risk of climate catastrophe. Instead it is the renewed economic strategy Britain needs to enjoy many more good jobs and revitalised economic growth. These arguments coexist with other claims that the net zero transition poses a huge risk to growth, with the regulation or investment it requires seen as holding back the recovery from the pandemic.[57]

Both claims should be taken with a pinch of salt, although the former is a better guide for policy makers given that any new route to achieving sustainably stronger economic growth will need a commitment to net zero at its core.[58] The transition will bring big benefits: not only helping avert climate disaster but improving air quality[59] and reducing our exposure to volatile energy costs.[60] The UK also has innovative strengths that can be built upon to supply the growing global demand for clean technologies, goods, and services.[61] And weaker regional economies are likely to benefit most from the

56 A Eyles & L E Major, What do school closures mean for social mobility?, Economics Observatory, January 2021.

57 R Clark, The Government's absurd commitment to net zero is impoverishing the nation, The Telegraph, March 2022.

58 N Stern & A Valero, Innovation, growth and the transition to net-zero emissions, Research Policy 50(9), November 2021.

59 A Corlett & J Marshall, Shrinking footprints: The impacts of the net zero transition on households and consumption, Resolution Foundation, March 2022.

60 Department for Business, Energy & Industrial Strategy, British energy security strategy, April 2022.

61 B Curran et al., Growing clean: Identifying and investing in sustainable growth opportunities across the UK, Resolution Foundation, May 2022.

expansion of green technologies: while overall innovation is concentrated in the South East, the parts of the country with the highest proportion of green patents include Derbyshire, Nottinghamshire, Lincolnshire, Tees Valley, and Durham.[62]

But the net zero transition's main macroeconomic effect in the short term is neither to significantly increase or reduce the level of GDP, but instead to change its composition by raising investment and lowering consumption (either today, if we forego consumption to invest, or tomorrow if we borrow for it). In the short term the transition is best seen as a significant invest-to-save process, as we pay in the coming years for the new infrastructure needed to allow us to heat our homes and travel without burning hydrocarbons.[63] This will not be a major boost to growth in the short term because it involves replacing large parts of our capital stock rather than adding to it. In the longer term that infrastructure will be cheaper to run, overwhelmingly because of electric vehicles, and if net zero-driven technological change leads to abundant, secure, and cheap electricity generation that would provide a major boost to growth.[64] But an economic strategy cannot come down to counting on the latter materialising during the 2020s.

Overall, net zero cannot be relied upon to deliver an economic silver bullet, and nor should we expect silver linings to Brexit or the pandemic to transform Britain's economic geography or its productivity.

We should not be counting on the change of the 2020s to catapult the UK out of stagnation

Instead of solving our economic problems, or exposing the UK to 1980s levels of labour market change, what has become clearer as we have delved deeper into these big changes as part of the Economy 2030 Inquiry is that the main result of these shocks considered together will be to reinforce the key challenge Britain is already wrestling with: stagnation. Change therefore is not the solution to our woes. Instead, Chapter Three wrestles with how to design a renewed economic strategy that can lift the UK from prolonged stagnation.

---

62 B Curran et al., Growing clean: Identifying and investing in sustainable growth opportunities across the UK, Resolution Foundation, May 2022.

63 Climate Change Committee, Sixth Carbon Budget, December 2020.

64 A Corlett & J Marshall, Shrinking footprints: The impacts of the net zero transition on households and consumption, Resolution Foundation, March 2022.

Chapter Three

The case for a new strategy

Chapter summary

- The magnitude of Britain's economic challenges means that the task of the 2020s is to renew our economic strategy to tackle low growth and high inequality.

- As well as being clear about the problems it must address, an effective strategy would start from the reality of our existing economy, identify real as well as surmountable constraints, be clear about trade offs, and be backed up by policies capable of moving the dial over the long term.

- Elements of a way forward have been proposed, from the UK Government's focus on science, to the Labour Party's green investment plans, or the Welsh Government's prioritisation of social partnership. And we can learn from international examples of countries who have renewed their economic strategies: for example Germany after unification.

- But we are not on course to renew our economic strategy. Partly because it is hard and partly because it is far from clear that policy makers are serious about doing so.

- Some argue we don't need growth because it won't translate into gains for ordinary households, ignoring the reality that a lack of growth is the cause of flatlining wages. More common is to recognise that growth is necessary, or that inequality is too high, but to be deeply unserious about what it might take to change things. A manufacturing jobs revival is promised, with no engagement with the reality of declines in such jobs across the advanced world. Half of the debate about Brexit denies its costs, while the other half denies its reality.

- There is a burning platform for a renewed economic strategy. People across the political spectrum are concerned about prolonged low growth and high inequality, but the task ahead is to be serious about the answers to it.

The previous chapters argued that the UK faces major challenges and changes in the 2020s. We now turn to how we should think about responding. The significance of the questions being asked means that the answers must amount to more than simple changes in policy here or there. Rather, the UK must renew its economic strategy and do so while focusing on the goals of sustainably higher growth, lower inequality, and successfully navigating change. We focus on the UK's economic strategy as a whole, although the analysis has significant implications for devolved nations and regions, who play important roles in supporting growth, reducing inequality and innovating on policy more generally.

The UK requires a renewed economic strategy

The longer Britain's position as a stagnation nation persists, the more dire the consequences will be for the country. This is clear for households: over the entire 20-year period to 2025-26, real typical household income growth was forecast at the time of the March 2022 Spring Statement to be just 9 per cent, whereas incomes would have increased by almost 50 per cent if they had risen at 2 per cent a year, which not so long ago was the norm.[1] This is also true for the state: even trying to maintain existing levels of public service provision requires a higher tax burden. And, more broadly, it also holds for the country as a whole: our place in the world and even the quality of our democracy may be at risk if stagnation becomes the new normal in the decades ahead.

Some take the view that there are specific policy shifts that can unlock a brighter future. The Prime Minister has talked of lower migration as being the key to a new high-wage economy,[2] while others view significant change on housing (be that planning liberalisation or a land value tax) as something of a silver bullet.[3]

There may be occasions when a single shift can address the major challenges facing a nation – such as when a macroeconomic policy mistake needs to be reversed in the case of Britain's withdrawal from the Gold Standard in 1931.

1 Calculated based on income projections as published in: T Bell et al., Inflation Nation: Putting Spring Statement 2022 in context, Resolution Foundation, March 2022.

2 Conservatives, Boris Johnson's keynote speech – We're getting on with the job, 6 October 2021.

3 S Bowman et al., The housing theory of everything, work in progress, September 2021.

But the 2020s is not one of those occasions. A wider renewal of our economic strategy, or a new route map to economic success, is required for at least three reasons.

First, the challenges the UK faces are huge in scale and diverse in nature. A tweak to the benefits system will not end a situation where low-income Brits are 22 per cent poorer than their French equivalents.[4] Investing in new green technologies is absolutely critical for the country, but on its own its impact would be far too small to generate strong growth for the UK economy as a whole.

Second, these challenges and changes – persistent low growth, high inequality, the shocks of Brexit and Covid-19, and the net zero transition – are heavily interdependent. Britain's approach to post-Brexit trade, not just to surface vehicle decarbonisation, will affect how large the country's emerging electric vehicle industry will be. The role of the public sector in delivering net zero, and incentivising business investment, will inevitably compete with other pressures on the public finances. There are, of course, always interdependencies for policy makers to consider, but in the decade ahead they are particularly acute and require different components of policy to be fully integrated.

Third, the upheaval of recent shocks has itself upended major planks of the country's prevailing economic strategy, while some of the longstanding challenges we currently face stem from its inadequacies. Brexit has disrupted a central pillar of traditional UK economic policy that has existed for the last half century: prioritising open access to a large, highly integrated, home market. Financial services were seen as the key component of Britain's comparative advantage in the world, but far less so after the financial crisis. And the traditional approach to economic policy has itself been found wanting in important respects. Large and persistent gaps between people and places (outlined in Chapter One) understandably led many to question whether it was fit for purpose in the first place.

---

4 See Figure **11**.

Economic strategies require goal orientation, an understanding of context, realism about trade offs, scale, and staying power

What are the key characteristics of successful economic strategies? Our assessment of the nature of the challenge ahead, informed by international experience as well as the UK's past, suggest there are five principal requirements.

1. ***Clear objectives***: a strategy must be clear about the problem it is trying to solve. We have made the case that our central problem is stagnation, defined as persistent low growth and longstanding high inequality. The challenge for the 2020s is generating stronger, sustainable, and inclusive growth.

2. ***Clarity about context***: good strategies don't start with a blank sheet of paper, but nor should they be entirely driven by the status quo. They need a clear recognition of context and an understanding of the opportunities and constraints based on a hard-headed assessment of the country's strengths and weaknesses. There should be no space for wishful, or nostalgic, thinking.

   This inevitably involves judgements about which aspects of the structure of the UK economy are deemed very hard to shift as opposed to those that are more malleable. Some path dependencies will inevitably form the backdrop to any strategy, but there will also be long-established economic patterns – whether in production, consumption, or distribution – that are susceptible to concerted policy action. Our commitment to the net zero transition, for instance, inevitably means that some parts of our economy will have to function very differently in the future, despite that involving disruptive change.

   We must also be realistic about what lies beyond domestic policy makers' control in a rich but medium-sized economy. Many key variables – whether commodity and energy prices, the technological frontier, or long-term interest rates – are set at the global level. And, as should be obvious to all after recent years, it is important to be aware that the UK is, and will remain, subject to global shocks.

3. ***Realism about trade offs***: recognition of trade offs is central to building a strategy rather than a wish list. They often exist between competing objectives: for example, when agglomeration effects create a tension between higher or more geographically balanced output.

   Resource constraints are central drivers of trade offs. This is usually thought of narrowly in terms of the public finances (tax versus spend, or one spending priority versus another), but it also applies more broadly to resource allocation across the economy as a whole. For example, the major increase in the numbers of workers that will undertake home retrofitting as implied by Government plans must come from somewhere. Likewise, boosting investment must, at least in the short run, mean lower consumption or higher net imports and hence foreign borrowing. All too often, trade offs such as these are brushed over.

   An economic strategy also inevitably raises wider political economy questions that require choices to be made, such as striking a balance between economic integration and national policy autonomy.

   The job of a strategy is not to resolve all trade offs in a simple binary fashion – not least because the job of politics in a democracy is to manage tensions that are often longstanding feature of societies and economies. But it must be honest about the existence of trade offs, clear about the balance that a strategy aims to strike between them, and open about the grounds for reaching this judgement. Without this approach, every policy decision inevitably involves either relitigating those trade offs or attempting to ignore them entirely, with downsides to a given decision papered over rather than addressed. Relatedly, all strategies must set priorities, which inevitably means being clear about what will not be done.

4. ***Sufficient scale***: having set out clear objectives and a route map towards achieving them, a strategy must be backed up by policies of sufficient scale that they can plausibly move the dial towards the desired outcome. In some times and places this may not require an ambitious set of policy proposals, but the diagnoses set out in the previous chapters suggests that, to have the necessary impact, a high-voltage policy response will be necessary in the current UK context.

5. ***Staying power***: to be effective an economic strategy must persist. Indeed, endemic policy and institutional short-termism has long beset UK policy making and is argued to have been a key weakness of the UK model over much of the 20th century.[5] It still afflicts us today, as evidenced, for example, through the short lifespan of the recently axed Industrial Strategy Council.[6] Stability and staying power is easier in some eras than others – and in some countries than others, reflecting the nature of their political systems and institutional settlements. Simplistic calls to 'take the politics out' of taking significant decisions are often misguided. But building long-termism into decision making via institutions that help reinforce it (such as the UK's National Infrastructure Commission), as well as the involvement of broader groups of stakeholders, can go some way to reducing the turbulence of winner-takes-all politics.

Economic strategies have been renewed before, in the UK and elsewhere

Some may look at these different components of an economic strategy, contrast it with the UK's recent experience, and conclude that it is not achievable. Certainly, countries can spend decades without such a strategy in place. And there is no blueprint from abroad or from our past that we should seek to replicate. But recent history, both here and elsewhere, does offer lessons to be learned (a series of forthcoming essays for the Economy 2030 Inquiry will explore these in detail).

The German experience after reunification is a prime example of a country navigating a big shock in a strategic fashion. The equivalent of more than £74 billion was spent on reunification every year (on average) between 1990 and 2018.[7] With cross-party consensus on doing 'whatever it takes' involving the near immediate harmonisation of social security and pension entitlements, huge support for public infrastructure in the East, alongside the modernisation of the antiquated capital stock of private sector businesses, focused particularly on the manufacturing sector. As a result, although there have been significant challenges, including East–West migration as well as a sluggish

5 N Crafts, Chapter in Economy 2030 Inquiry international case studies book, Resolution Foundation, forthcoming.

6 The Industrial Strategy Council was launched in November 2018 and abolished in March 2021: M Kleinman, Kwarteng axes star-studded Industrial Strategy Council with hint at BEIS rebranding, Sky News, March 2021.

7 K Enenkel & F Rösel, Chapter in Economy 2030 Inquiry international case studies book, Resolution Foundation, forthcoming.

move in the East towards knowledge-based sectors, both productivity and incomes gaps fell significantly between East and West.

New Zealand also experienced a major economic shock when the UK decided to join the European Economic Community in 1972, significantly reducing access to the nation's largest export market. This shift, together with the energy upheavals of the 1970s, had major political and economic ramifications and resulted in long-term changes in the economy's industrial and sectoral mix, as well as a reorientation of export markets. After an initial period of instability and repeated crisis, governments led by both main parties were involved in a far-reaching shift in the prevailing economic model, embracing a major programme of market liberalisation, a floating exchange rate, radical public service reform, and a new macroeconomic regime that defined much of the late 1980s and 1990s. It was a highly controversial experiment. These structural changes in the economy and the prevailing policy model were associated with a sharp rise in inequality from the late 1980s to 2000 and a major shift in the balance of power within the workplace as union membership rates fell sharply.[8] Arguably, aspects of the programme of the current Ardern administration – such as proposed reforms to the system of industrial relations via sector-based Fair Pay Agreements – are an attempt to rebalance some of the consequences of the shifts that characterised the 1980s and 1990s.[9]

Just as important as the lessons from conscious efforts to reset aspects of an economic strategy are the stark warnings from countries that have failed to address underlying weaknesses. Italy stands out in this regard. In the late 20th century, Italy was widely viewed as an affluent, high-skilled European economy. Indeed, aspects of its model, such as its vibrant networks of export-oriented small and medium-sized artisanal firms, were held up as a system of industrial organisation that other economies should emulate.[10] Yet, remarkably, Italian total factor productivity was actually lower immediately before the pandemic than it was two decades earlier. Multiple reinforcing factors are argued to have underpinned this long-term stagnation, including the large proportion of small unproductive firms and lack of business dynamism; poor innovation systems and workplace skills; and repeated concerns over fiscal sustainability.[11] Political

8 C Ball & J Creedy, Inequality in New Zealand 1983/84 to 2013/14, New Zealand Treasury, June 2015.

9 For a full assessment, see: A Grimes, Chapter in Economy 2030 Inquiry international case studies book, Resolution Foundation, forthcoming.

10 M Piore & C Sabel, The Second Industrial Divide: Possibilities for Prosperity, Basic Books, 1984.

11 L Codogno & G Galli, Chapter in Economy 2030 Inquiry international case studies book, Resolution Foundation, forthcoming.

instability and increased polarisation were both a symptom and partial cause of these problems. Clearly the Italian context is very different to the UK's, but it serves as a salutary example of the risk that once stagnation becomes entrenched it can be hard to reverse.

In Box 7 we discuss two examples of more strategic approaches to economic policy making by post-war Prime Ministers: Wilson and Thatcher.

Box 7: Examples of economic strategy from post-war Prime Ministers

Economic strategies have existed in Britain's recent past, and insights can also be gleaned from these periods in modern British history.

Harold Wilson's Government came to power in 1964 committed to achieving faster economic growth which, in Wilson's view, relied on a reorientation of industrial and social policy. The core objective was the rapid expansion of rising industries and the reallocation of skilled labour towards them. This shift required the existence of an appropriate 'social infrastructure' to help smooth the path for transitioning workers. Seen through this lens, flat-rate welfare benefits appeared to be an impediment to workers, particularly skilled workers, embracing risk, and indeed risked a counter-reaction to the prospect of industrial change. The task was to "ease the transition from job to job which must be made if the country is to achieve the redeployment of manpower which it so urgently needs".[12] The necessary social infrastructure, as Wilson saw it, included a shift towards earnings-related and time-limited unemployment benefits. Alongside this came a raft of other measures aimed in different ways at supporting labour to adjust: the Statutory Redundancy Pay Act (1966), the delivery of Industrial Training Boards, the pioneering of the polytechnic system, the expansion of universities, and the launch of the Open University. The intention – even if eventually overshadowed by the 1967 devaluation crisis and related economic challenges – was that social security, workforce development, together with wider industrial policy, were to be considered (to a degree at least) in the round.

The next post-war Government arriving in office with clear strategic instincts about the

12 G Kelly, Preparing for a decade of economic change: Lessons from the era of White Heat, Resolution Foundation, July 2021.

direction of economic policy was Mrs Thatcher's administration. The goal of creating a flexible labour market was seen as a driver of a more dynamic, service-oriented economy, and it sat alongside emerging plans for financial deregulation and privatisation. Labour market reform was thought to be a necessary step in reducing unemployment (which peaked at almost 12 per cent in 1984) and dovetailed with the industrial (and political) objective of reducing trade union power.

The Thatcher governments cut the replacement rate of benefits for the unemployed relative to average wages and brought in a series of wider reforms: wages councils were weakened and then abolished, trade union power was reduced, the tax burden was shifted towards consumption and away from high marginal rates of income tax, and self-employment and entrepreneurship were supported. These measures, together with the wider industrial restructuring of the era, resulted in high levels of job mobility between sectors, strong average income growth, and rapidly rising wage differentials, contributing to soaring inequality. Elevated levels of unemployment persisted throughout most of the 1980s, with particularly high concentrations in mining and industrial towns whose long-term futures were profoundly changed. All told, it amounted to an economic strategy that altered the trajectory of the UK economy and had consequences – for good and ill – that the country is still grappling with four decades later.

Potential components of a renewed strategy are being debated but crisis response has dominated policy making

While few would claim that the UK has a clearly established economic strategy as it emerges from the pandemic, the question of the future direction of our economy and need for a plan to revitalise growth is at least a feature of current policy and political debates.

Key figures on both sides of the political spectrum are raising the salience of prolonged low growth:

> *"Because when the economy and our standard of living are not growing fast enough, consent for the system is undermined. If we cannot accelerate growth, people will begin to lose faith in the moral and material case for free markets...So, the question we face today is urgent and it is consequential: How do we accelerate growth, and, in doing so, restore people's faith in the free market?"*[13]
>
> (Rishi Sunak)

> *"We are now in the worst of all possible worlds, with inflation high and rising, and growth low and falling – in other words, there is stagflation...Growth has stagnated, not just this year but over the last 12 years."*[14]
>
> (Rachel Reeves)

The ideas and commitments currently being developed may not add up to a comprehensive approach, but some of them will certainly be useful ingredients for a renewed strategy. There is much to build on, both from national government approaches and from the different strategies and policy directions being pursued within devolved governments. Examples include:

- The UK punches above its weight in the field of science, ranking first among the G7 in citation impact and producing 14 per cent of the world's most highly cited publications.[15] The Government has identified this as one source of comparative advantage and high-tech spillovers for the UK economy,[16] with an ambition to cement the UK's status as a 'science superpower'.[17] Relatedly, the Government intends to increase public R&D funding by 25 per cent (in real terms) between 2022-23 and 2024-25.[18]

---

13 R Sunak, Chancellor Rishi Sunak's Mais Lecture 2022, February 2022.

14 R Reeves, Speech in House of Commons debate: Achieving economic growth, May 2022.

15 Department for Business, Energy & Industrial Strategy, International comparison of the UK research base, 2019: Accompanying note, July 2019.

16 Department for Business, Energy & Industrial Strategy, UK Innovation Strategy: Leading the future by creating it, July 2021.

17 J Madingley & P Vallance, The UK as a science and technology superpower, Council for Science and Technology, June 2021.

18 HM Treasury, Autumn Budget and Spending Review 2021, October 2021.

- That increased funding forms part of the sustained increase in public investment that is currently underway. The Government plans to raise public sector net investment to a steady state level of 2.5 per cent of GDP from 2024-25, up from 1.9 per cent of GDP in 2019-20.[19] This increase in public capital spending will contribute to raising the UK's low overall rate of investment, which the Government has recognised is holding the UK's economy back.[20]

- The UK has an unusual, and very welcome, degree of cross-party consensus on the objective of reaching net zero greenhouse gas emissions by 2050 and there is broad-based support for the central role decarbonisation should play in attempts to strengthen the UK economy via a 'green industrial revolution'. The net zero target is enshrined in law, with more detailed mechanisms to support the delivery of the transition and accountability for it (via the Climate Change Committee) than are seen in most similar countries.

- The UK's departure from the EU, and lack of an imminent prospect of a trade deal with our second largest trading partner – the United States – has seen the UK Government seek to affect a 'tilt' towards the Indo-Pacific. While the region lacks geographical proximity, it includes a set of countries (prominently India) with which trade costs are currently relatively high and that are expected to experience rapid growth in imports, including for products that the UK specialises in.[21] However, it remains to be seen whether a material liberalisation in trade with the Indo-Pacific region is possible, and what the side effects of any reciprocal liberalisation of imports may be for the Government's other objectives. Brexit has also seen the UK regain full control of migration policy and introduce a new regime. This is likely to have the effect of increasing the average skill level of migrants to the UK somewhat, at the cost of making the UK workforce less flexible in response to economic shocks.[22] However, the overall impact of the new regime is likely to be small, and certainly will not by itself raise productivity and wages materially.[23]

---

19 OBR, Public Finance Databank, April 2022.

20 R Sunak, Chancellor Rishi Sunak's Mais Lecture 2022, February 2022.

21 S Hale, A presage to India: Assessing the UK's new Indo-Pacific trade focus, Resolution Foundation, January 2022.

22 K Henehan, Under new management: How immigration policy change will, and won't, affect the UK's path to becoming a high-wage, high-productivity economy, Resolution Foundation, February 2022.

23 T Bell, There is no simple story of migrants down, wages up: The UK needs a post-Brexit, post-Covid economic strategy, not another argument about immigration, Resolution Foundation, October 2021.

- The Government published a White Paper on 'Levelling Up' in February 2022, which was concerned with the important objective of reducing the UK's relatively high levels of geographic inequality.[24] This paper recognised that a change in policy regime would be necessary to bring this about, and set ambitious and measurable medium-term goals, 12 of which are intended to be enshrined in legislation. This legislation also set out an enabling legal framework for further English devolution, which may facilitate a wider adoption of the mayoral-led Combined Authority model being pioneered in city regions. However, in some places these targets are unrealistic or not well defined.[25] For example, the regions of the UK do not seem to be populous enough for each of them to have a globally competitive city as planned.

- The UK's unique structure of four sovereign nations, each with their own culture, history and governance provides an opportunity for experimentation with strategy and policy, as well as different approaches to economic leadership and strategy to emerge. The Scottish Government recently published its 10-year economic strategy,[26] fusing a focus on the net zero transition, and the specific growth opportunities that Scotland is well-placed to take advantage of, with ambitions for a 'wellbeing economy' and significant reductions in poverty.[27] Meanwhile, the Welsh Parliament is considering legislation that seeks to increase the involvement of trade unions in the decisions made by public bodies via various routes, including the establishment of a 'Social Partnership Council', comprised of government, employer and worker representatives, to advise the Welsh Government on policies in relation to fair work, procurement and well-being.[28]

Despite a number of these ideas representing significant policy developments, they are not cohesively joined up and, more broadly, the UK has not fundamentally renewed its pre-financial crisis economic strategy. Austerity was the focus of governments for much of the 2010s, but despite several central components of the pre-financial crisis approach being challenged or

---

24 Department for Levelling Up, Housing and Communities, Levelling up the United Kingdom, February 2022.

25 E Shearer, Will the levelling up missions help reduce regional inequality?, Institute for Government, March 2022.

26 Scottish Government, Scotland's National Strategy for Economic Transformation, March 2022.

27 Legislation.gov.uk, Child Poverty (Scotland) Act 2017.

28 Hannah Blythyn MS, Written Statement: Introduction of Social Partnership and Public Procurement (Wales) Bill, June 2022.

entirely altered over the past decade and a half, no broader renewal has taken place. This is certainly a problem, though it is not entirely surprising given that the dominant form of economic policy making during this period has been crisis management.

Major innovation in or rethinking of economic policy during this period has come in the form of improvisation in the face of those crises, rather than via new strategic thinking. UK policy makers certainly responded with impressive agility and speed in some areas, from bank nationalisation at the height of the financial crisis to furlough at the start of the pandemic. But the seriousness with which emergency action was taken during these crises has not been matched by a seriousness of purpose when it comes to longer-term questions regarding how the UK builds a path to economic success.

Ultimately, the UK is not on course to renew our economic strategy because we are not serious about the task

We should not be confident that the UK is on course to renew its economic strategy because we are collectively not serious about doing so. While there are broad-based rhetorical commitments to focusing on raising growth and reducing inequality, we are not hard-headed enough about the scale and nature of the sustained action required to make a significant difference to either. Nor are we seriously grappling with the constraints imposed by the nature of global and domestic economies and how they should affect the choices we make.

Some even say we don't need growth, in part because they claim it won't translate into gains for ordinary households. This ignores the vital point that it is the very lack of productivity that has driven our post-financial crisis wage stagnation.[29]

The far more common approach, though, is to want growth but not be serious about how to achieve it. Politicians often talk as if they will reorient the UK's economy towards goods, driving a manufacturing jobs revival. But this aspiration fails to engage with the clear trend towards a decline in such jobs across the advanced world, reflecting the fact that advanced manufacturing is

29 M Whittaker, Dead-end relationship? Exploring the link between productivity and workers' living standards, Resolution Foundation, January 2020. N Oulton, The Productivity-Welfare Linkage: A Decomposition, ESCoE Discussion Paper 2022-07, March 2022.

high productivity, in no small part because it is not job rich.[30] In short, far too much of the rhetorical debate about the future of our economy has become unmoored from the underlying reality of the British economy.

Another version of this tendency relates to Brexit. For some, the facts about certain negative impacts that Brexit has had on our economy cannot be admitted, which is the prior stage to addressing them. Equally, many who saw net benefits to the UK staying within the EU are reluctant to engage with the political and legal facts of our departure, including the remote prospect of them changing over the medium term. Others claim that either much lower, or higher, migration will solve our ills despite there being little evidence for either proposition.[31] Meanwhile, the policy-making community spent much of the past decade worrying about robots taking all of our jobs, even as business investment – a precondition to getting some technological advancement – flatlined. And much of our public discourse is predicated on the belief that it is a problem for the British economy that change is permanently speeding up precisely at a time when we are experiencing the lowest rate of structural industrial change since at least the 1930s.[32]

It's not just when it comes to achieving growth where we are falling short. The same applies to inequality. While the basic questions of fairness posed by the large gaps between people and places are recognised, we are equally lacking in seriousness when it comes to what it would take to answer this. Our local authorities are busy bidding for small sums of Levelling Up investment, while decades of much larger sums would be required to make a dent in the capital stock deficits of underperforming cities outside London.[33] Similarly, discussions of inclusive prosperity too often collapse into firms' promises about greater corporate social responsibility or taking environmental, social, and governance (ESG) issues seriously, while workers have no right to a minimum notice periods for their shifts. When it comes to raising taxes, we turn to National Insurance despite knowing that it falls disproportionately on the shoulders of those whose wages have flatlined. A successful strategy requires long-term commitment, whereas the UK today is characterised by

30 E Chappell, Starmer pledges to reverse "shocking" manufacturing decline caused by Tories, LabourList, 14 February 2022; George Osborne promised a "march of the makers" in his 2011 Budget, 23 Mar 2011.

31 K Henehan, Under new management: How immigration policy change will, and won't, affect the UK's path to becoming a high-wage, high-productivity economy, Resolution Foundation, February 2022.

32 N Cominetti et al., Changing jobs? Change in the UK labour market and the role of worker mobility, Resolution Foundation, January 2022.

33 P Brandily et al., Bridging the gap: What would it take to narrow the UK's productivity disparities, Resolution Foundation, June 2022.

short-termism (for example cutting home insulation measures by 90 per cent in the early 2010s even as we recommitted to a net zero future).[34]

These are not the hallmarks of a nation that is serious about the task of renewing its economic strategy to meet the challenge of new times or the inheritance of low growth and high inequality that we carry into the 2020s.

Developing a successful economic strategy is far from easy

Even if we were taking the task of renewing the UK's economic strategy seriously as a country, it would be hard work to deliver. And it is important to recognise that even in tranquil times, the task is easier to consider from the safety of think-tanks and universities than amid the daily demands of politics, let alone in a period of seemingly continual crisis.

This is why the Economy 2030 Inquiry has been structured in a particular way. Our work represents a two-year partnership of academics and policy experts, first establishing relevant facts about both the present and the future, and then pivoting towards strategic policy making with significant deliberative engagement with the public. Our aim is to outline an economic strategy that has the characteristics listed above and offers the UK a route to economic success in the world as we find it, not as we would like it to be. In the following chapter, we start to identity the outlines of what a plausible national economic strategy might look like. The case for such a renewal of the nation's approach is clear – in the longer term the status quo is neither economically or democratically sustainable.

34 S Cran-McGreehin, Households are paying the price for slow progress on insulating homes, Energy & Climate Intelligence Unit, January 2022.

Chapter Four

Rebooting Britain

Chapter summary

- The UK is the second-largest services exporter in the world and a broad-based services economy, built on successful musicians and architects as well as bankers. This is not the cause of our slow growth: services-led economies are on average higher-income than goods specialists.
- This will not change anytime soon: of the top 10 products the UK was most specialised in back in 1989, seven were in our top 10 in 2019.
- The task for Britain is to make a success of our services economy, including by wrestling with the upward pressure it places on inequality: jobs in tradable services are 80 per cent more likely than average to pay in the top 5 per cent while services exports are concentrated in the highest wage areas.
- While our current economic specialisation is consistent with future prosperity, our regional divides are not. The UK's most plausible route to raising national income and closing regional gaps is our big cities outside London succeeding: all of England's biggest cities outside London currently have productivity levels below the national average.
- But achieving this requires change on a scale not currently contemplated: halving Manchester's productivity gap to London, so that it becomes as productive as Edinburgh, would require tens of billions of pounds of investment and an increase in size of over 500,000 workers.
- The 2020s has to be a high-investment decade not just because of net zero, but because the UK has been a low-investment economy for too long. In the 40 years to 2019, total fixed investment in the UK averaged 19 per cent of GDP, the lowest in the G7.
- We need an economy better able to manage change. In the UK, 40 per cent of employed people experience a large loss of income when becoming non-employed, compared to 30 per cent of employed people in Germany and 26 per cent of employed people in France. This lack of income insurance not only provides too little support to those losing a job, but prevents risk taking.

- Good jobs must be an explicit objective of an economic strategy. We should celebrate the benefits of our flexible labour market, including low unemployment, but not be scared of tackling its flaws. Half of shift workers in Britain receive less than a week's notice of their working hours or schedules, and under 10 per cent of low-paid private sector workers are unionised.

- We should combine realism about the different roles of different places in our economy with an ambition to reject wide gaps in status and quality of life across the country. Delivering on that ambition is hard when council revenues per person fell by 30 per cent between 2009 and 2019 in the most-deprived places, compared to 15 per cent in the least-deprived places. The proportion of people thinking their local area has deteriorated in the preceding two years has risen steadily from 20 per cent in 2013-14 to 26 per cent in 2019-20.

- The British state has grown which, combined with slow growth, has seen taxes raised to their highest levels since the 1940s. But these higher taxes will need to be fair and efficient. Both main parties' focus on raising National Insurance has asked more of younger workers at a time of flatlining wages, but nothing of landlords or most pensioners. A strategy for the 2020s will need to consider new approaches, recognising that wealth has risen from three to almost eight times national income since the 1980s, while wealth taxes have not risen at all as a share of GDP.

Renewing our economic strategy

We have argued that the task facing Britain in the 2020s is to renew our economic strategy to tackle the twin challenges of low growth and high inequality, and to do so in a period of more significant change than we have been used to. It is far from certain that our politics will rise to this task: it is not an easy undertaking, and it remains unclear whether we are serious as a nation about confronting it.

This chapter turns to what the key building blocks of a more serious attempt might look like: one that is grounded in the evidence about the kind of economy the UK is and could plausibly be. It aims to be serious not just about the constraints and trade offs involved but also the scale of ambition required to make a substantial difference. Its argument is that there is a plausible landing zone for the kind of strategy that is needed, which offers the prospect not just of overcoming our problems but of building on our strengths to set the UK on a path to being a fairer, more prosperous, and greener country.

Intentionally our focus is on the most material elements of a renewed UK-wide strategy, rather than a comprehensive list of every policy area. The second phase of The Economy 2030 Inquiry over the coming year will develop specific policy interventions that would be required to make the implementation of such a strategy a success.

Getting serious about the nature of the UK economy: a broad-based services superpower

A foundational aspect of an economic strategy is clarity about what kind of economy it relates to, given that this underpins everything from the big picture of how growth is achieved and shared, to the specific policy choices a strategy might imply (for example, what should be prioritised in post-Brexit trade agreements).

It doesn't take a long time studying economic data to see that for the UK this starting point is our strength as a broad-based services economy. The view that our economy is narrowly built on banking is as misplaced as the claim that there is an easy route to turning ourselves into a German-style manufacturing powerhouse.

Services account for almost half of UK exports (45 per cent, or $418 billion),[1] which is roughly twice the OECD average share (Figure 26) and the clear majority of our trade in terms of value added.[2] Although it is rarely celebrated, the UK is in fact the second largest exporter of services in the world, behind only the US.

Figure 26: Services account for almost half of UK exports, roughly twice the OECD average

Goods and services exports and imports as a proportion of GDP: OECD & UK

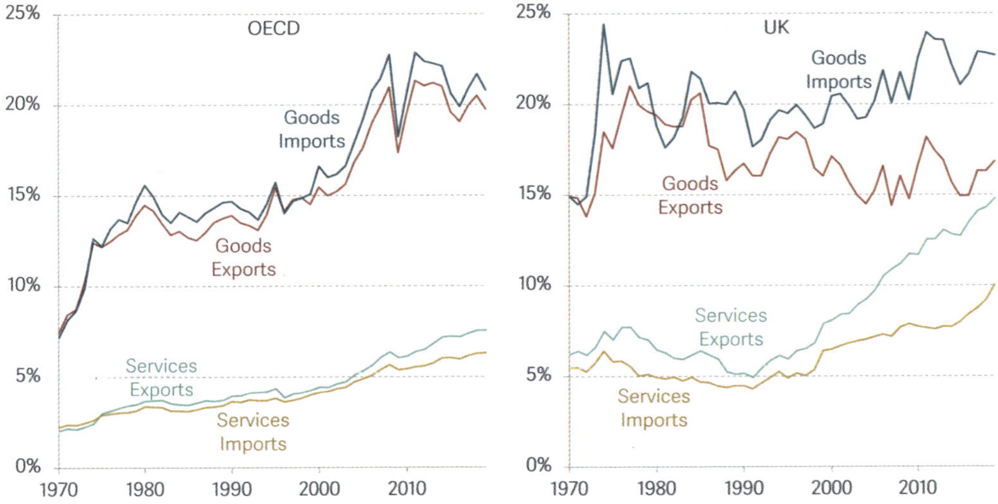

Notes: The set of countries included in the OECD excludes those with missing data over the period.
Source: World Bank, Trade and Services Exports and Imports as a Proportion of GDP.

The UK's comparative advantages stretch across a broad range of high-value tradable services – not only banking and finance, whose proportion of total exports in fact fell from 12 per cent in 2009 to 9 per cent in 2019, but information and communications, cultural, and intellectual property services too.[3] When combined with important, but more concentrated, strengths in certain goods sectors, such as beverages and aerospace (see Box 8), our overall degree of export specialisation is typical for a country of our size and level of development. The UK is far from a one-trick pony.

1 J De Lyon et al., Enduring strengths: Analysing the UK's current and potential economic strengths, and what they mean for its economic strategy, at the start of the decisive decade, Resolution Foundation, April 2022.

2 Services excluding construction contribute 63 per cent of value added as a proportion of total value added, see: OECD, Trade in Value Added (TiVA), Principal Indicators, 2021.

3 Analysis of ONS, UK Trade in Services; UK Trade in Goods.

Box 8: The role of manufacturing

Recognising that the UK's economy is, and will remain, a services-led economy should not mean giving up on manufacturing: it is not an either/or situation with the UK having significant, albeit concentrated, manufacturing strengths to build on and these often being highly complementary with related services.

The UK currently specialises in pharmaceuticals (as part of the wider life sciences sector), as well as beverages and aerospace.[4] Understanding what we are already good at as a nation is important to supporting future areas of strength that are likely to be closely aligned to existing capabilities. Our analysis indicates that potential manufacturing opportunities for the UK are clustered in the chemicals and machinery categories – including the production of medical equipment. The UK's specialisms in 'clean' technologies could also be built upon, with the UK within the top 10 exporters of 'green products'.[5]

Supporting our existing manufacturing strengths, and building new ones, will be central tasks for a renewed economic strategy. But more weight cannot be placed on manufacturing within the strategy than it can plausibly bear. For example, claims that it can be a main driver of high-quality, high-paying jobs growth are overdone. The entirety of manufacturing now accounts for just 8 per cent of employment in the UK and the parts of manufacturing likely to grow after Brexit are lower paying (e.g. food manufacturing).

A plausible economic strategy should be grounded in the UK economy remaining services-dominated

If the UK is to thrive during the 2020s it will be by making a success of these existing industrial strengths – embracing as well as adding to them – and ensuring more people and places enjoy the benefits from such an approach. The alternative – of basing a renewed strategy on attempting a significant industrial transformation (as some leading politicians, at least rhetorically, are

4 J De Lyon et al., Enduring strengths: Analysing the UK's current and potential economic strengths, and what they mean for is economic strategy at the start of the decisive decade, Resolution Foundation, April 2022.

5 B Curran et al., Growing clean: Identifying and investing in sustainable growth opportunities across the UK, Resolution Foundation, May 2022.

keen to do) – is highly unlikely to be successful, in large part because it is very unlikely to happen.[6] If we are to succeed, it will be as a better version of Britain, not a British version of Germany.

Countries' industrial specialisations are highly persistent: the UK has been a services superpower for over four decades, and of the top 10 products in which the UK was most specialised in 1989, seven were also in our top 10 in 2019. Even a huge change like Brexit will not fundamentally change this, as discussed in Chapter Two. Attempting to transform the UK into a manufacturing-heavy economy would require huge investments (reflecting countries such as Germany and South Korea having materially larger stocks of physical and human capital) and lower consumption for years, with far from guaranteed success. Internationally, major swings between goods and services specialisation by advanced economies are extremely rare, reflecting the strong role of accumulated knowledge, capital, institutions, and experienced labour in being able to compete globally in high-value-added sectors that are central to maintaining our living standards.

Moreover, there are good reasons for the UK to build on what we already do well. Our industrial structure does not lie behind our weak economic performance: on average, services specialists like the UK are richer than manufacturing specialists. And our product mix is perfectly consistent with rapid export growth: global demand actually grew faster in our key export industries than in China's in the decade to 2019, but China's exports grew twice as fast.[7] India's demand for business services and telecommunication and computer services, two competitive UK export sectors, is expected to more than triple in real terms between 2019 and 2030.[8]

Our non-tradable sectors are central to an economic strategy, but are unlikely to be the main drivers of growth

Most goods and many services can be traded fairly cheaply over long distances within or between countries – think of sunflower oil, mobile phones, and song rights. For the rest, trade is too expensive or impractical, or is limited by the

6 George Osborne, House of Commons, Financial Statement, March 2011; J Elgot, Labour vows to reverse decline in UK manufacturing, The Guardian, February 2022.

7 J De Lyon et al., Enduring strengths: Analysing the UK's current and potential economic strengths, and what they mean for is economic strategy at the start of the decisive decade, Resolution Foundation, April 2022.

8 S Hale, A presage to India: Assessing the UK's new Indo-Pacific trade focus, Resolution Foundation, January 2022.

need for production and consumption to take place in the same location – think of fresh croissants or a haircut. Some have suggested that an economic strategy should approach growth by focusing on the latter (non-tradable) sectors rather than the former (tradable) sectors.[9] But such an approach would be misguided.

An economic strategy needs to focus on creating a bedrock of decent jobs in every place, as we turn to below. And good jobs in non-tradable sectors are foundational to such an approach – they account for 60 per cent of hours worked in the UK, and provide vital goods and services.[10] But these sectors should not be the central focus when it comes to raising growth and productivity.

In fact, aiming to increase the proportion of jobs in non-tradable sectors would reduce productivity in the economy overall: tradable industries are around 14 per cent more productive than non-tradable industries[11] which have a higher share of lower-paid jobs.[12] There are desirable ways to raise productivity in non-tradable sectors, but focusing efforts to raise productivity there may also be risky. Not only can such gains be hard, or undesirable, to realise (for example by reducing the delivery of face-to-face social care), but the main effects may be lower prices for higher-earning consumers while intensifying work for lower earners. We should pause before taking that approach to raising productivity, given that the proportion of workers who say their job requires that they work "very hard" is already high, having increased from 30 per cent in the early 1990s to 46 per cent pre-pandemic.[13]

Our goals instead should be to increase the employment proportion and productivity of tradable sectors while improving pay and conditions in non-tradable sectors, as Box 9 explores. This may involve higher prices (a subject we return to below).

9 R Reeves, The everyday economy, March 2018.

10 B Broadbent et al., The Brexit vote, productivity growth and macroeconomic adjustments in the United Kingdom, Bank of England, August 2019.

11 These two categories inevitably hide a huge amount of productivity variation within sectors and there are some kinds of non-tradables – such as health and education – that help to make the whole economy more productive, as well as being valuable in their own right. The figures on employment and productivity in the tradable and non-tradable sectors are taken from B Broadbent et al., The Brexit vote, productivity growth and macroeconomic adjustments in the United Kingdom, Bank of England, November 2020.

12 J De Lyon et al., Enduring strengths: Analysing the UK's current and potential economic strengths, and what they mean for its economic strategy, at the start of the decisive decade, Resolution Foundation, April 2022.

13 K Shah & D Tomlinson, Work experiences: Changes in the subjective experience of work, Resolution Foundation, September 2021.

Box 9: The implications of growing the tradable sectors

Shifting more workers into tradable sectors generally will tend to raise GDP somewhat on the basis of its higher productivity levels: boosting the proportion of hours in tradables by 5 percentage points – equal to the fall in the share between 1994 and 2018 – would increase aggregate productivity by 0.7 per cent. More significant gains would come from policy makers focusing on growing the size of higher productivity parts of the tradable sector and productivity levels across the sector.

Boosting employment in the tradables sector can help the economy more widely. For example, suppose that the economy consists only of car factories (tradable) and restaurants (non-tradable). If people move jobs from restaurants to (higher-paying) car factories, they will seek to spend more money going out for dinner. There are two possibilities at this point. Either the restaurants find a way to become more productive and serve more customers with fewer staff, boosting GDP and restaurant wages, or they don't, and the restaurants compete for waiting staff and raise their wages and prices to choke off the extra demand.

Recognising the nature of the UK economy is also important in tackling the challenges it brings

We need to understand the nature of our economy, not only to make a success of formulating and implementing an economic strategy, but also to address the downsides it brings. The key aspect to highlight is that tradable services, all else being equal, push up on inequality between people and places. In 2016-17, over half of the around 50,000 people in the top 0.1 per cent of the UK taxable income distribution worked in 'finance, insurance, and real estate' or were providing 'professional, scientific, and technical services'.[14] Moreover, as Figure 27 shows, while goods exports are fairly evenly spread across areas irrespective of local wage levels, services exports are much more concentrated in highly-productive areas accounting for 30 per cent of gross value added

14 M Brewer & C Samano Robles, Top incomes in the UK: analysis of the 2015-16 Survey of Personal Incomes, Institute for Social and Economic Research, 2019

(GVA) in the highest wage areas, compared to less than 15 per cent across the rest of the country.[15] And jobs in tradable services are 80 per cent more likely than average to pay in the top 5 per cent.[16]

Figure 27: Tradable services are concentrated in the highest-income regions of the UK

Goods and services exports as a proportion of gross value added (GVA) across regions grouped by real wage decile: UK, 2018

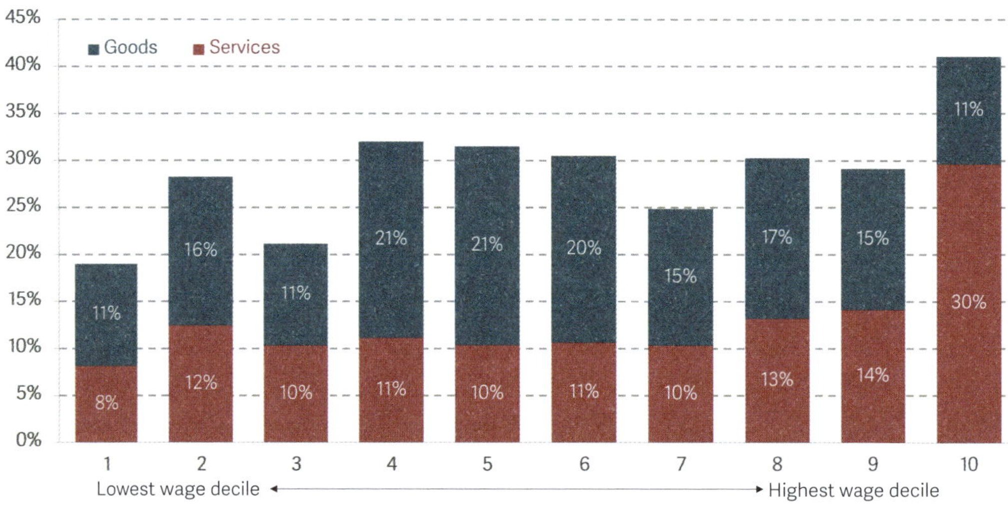

Notes: Each NUTS region is assigned to a real income decile based on regional average real wages in 2018. The share of services and trade is calculated as a share of GVA for that group of regions. Services excludes regions with no services trade data and Northern Irish regions for which no data available.
Source: Analysis of ONS, International Trade in Services by Subnational Areas of the UK; ONS, UK Regional Trade in Goods Statistics Disaggregated by Smaller Geographical Areas.

So action will be required to ensure that the benefits of the UK's trade specialisation are widely shared. This is clearly possible. France and the US specialise in services exports and are very productive, but the former has lower household inequality and the latter a better spread of productive places than the UK. Recognising the nature of our economy is not the same thing as welcoming all aspects of it, but an economic strategy that fails to understand it is no strategy at all.

15 J De Lyon et al., Trading places: Brexit and the path to longer-term improvements in living standards, Resolution Foundation, October 2021.

16 J De Lyon et al., Enduring strengths: Analysing the UK's current and potential economic strengths, and what they mean for its economic strategy, at the start of the decisive decade, Resolution Foundation, April 2022.

Getting serious about the constraints holding the economy back

A renewed economic strategy doesn't just need to be clear-eyed about our strengths, it also needs to put up in lights the big barriers that hold us back from making a success of the kind of economy we want to become.

This inevitably involves judgements about the extent to which these barriers are amenable to policy change. Unlike our biggest strength, our persistent and deep services specialisation, some major constraints can and should be shifted. Here we take the most salient barriers to widely shared economic prosperity in our services-led economy in turn: the UK's unbalanced economic geography, prolonged underinvestment in capital in all its forms, and the extent to which welfare policy and high housing costs prevent our economy from being as dynamic as it could be.

Ending the underperformance of major cities outside London is a national priority but requires change far beyond anything currently contemplated

UK economic spatial disparities are large. In 2019, London produced £76,000 of value added per job, more than twice that produced in Powys and Torbay.[17] And they are persistent: 60 per cent of the pre-pandemic variation in productivity across areas can be explained by the pattern in 2002, while 80 per cent of the variation in incomes across local authorities can be predicted by the pattern in 1997.

But while the starting point for an economic strategy should be to accept path dependency on our industrial structure, it must confront elements of it on economic geography. While our current economic specialisation is consistent with future prosperity, our regional gaps are not – as Michael Gove has noted, the UK is like a jumbo jet running mostly on one (London and the South East-shaped) engine.[18]

The services-led nature of our economy tells us what a plausible route to overcoming this problem will be. High value services industries thrive when similar firms co-locate in large places with highly educated populations: cities.

17 P Brandily et al., Bridging the gap: What would it take to narrow the UK's productivity disparities?, Resolution Foundation, June 2022.

18 M Gove, Britain's a jet plane that needs to be firing on all its engines...not just the one in the South East and London, The Mail on Sunday, January 2022.

Indeed, during the 21st century this pattern has been reinforced, along with the importance of an area's workforce size, skill levels, and stocks of capital (including intangibles) in determining its productivity growing.

Our large regional productivity gaps fundamentally reflect our failure to ensure that enough of our big cities, all deeply scarred by deindustrialisation, have successfully made the transition to contribute to our national success in tradable services. London alone accounts for 63 per cent of the UK's surplus in services trade, and aside from Edinburgh, the UK does not have any highly-productive mid-sized metro areas (see Figure 28).[19] The popular focus on lower productivity gaps between places in Germany offers little guide for the UK in the 2020s, with its more even spread of output reflecting a goods-dominated economy. But France, also a services-led economy, has more-productive second cities, like Lyon, which stand out relative to the likes of Birmingham and Manchester: Paris is only 26 per cent more productive than Lyon, whereas London is 41 per cent more productive than Manchester.

Figure 28: The UK's large cities are further behind the capital than in France

Gross value added (GVA) per worker by country and area: 2018

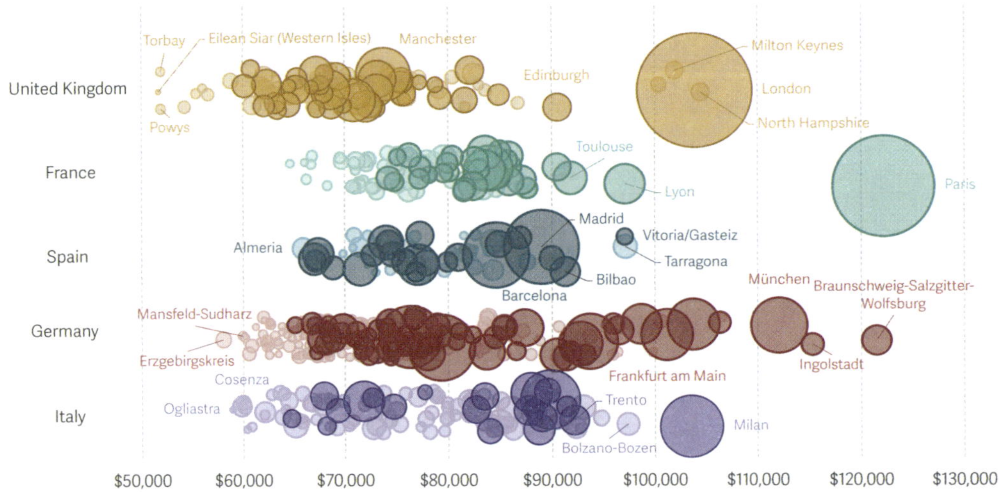

Notes: PPP adjusted. Spatial units are a combination of OECD metro regions and NUTS3 for non-metro regions. Metro areas are shown in darker bubbles in the figure. Bubbles are proportional to the number of workers in each region. Gross value added (GVA) is the value of a unit's outputs less the value of inputs used in the production process to produce the outputs.
Source: Analysis of OECD, Regional Economy Database.

19 ONS, International trade in services by subnational areas of the UK: 2018, September 2020.

Turning this around is certainly possible, with a welcome consensus emerging about the need to 'level up' our country and some major policy shifts (including a commitment to increase public R&D spending – an important enabler of economic growth – outside the Greater South East by 40 per cent between 2021-22 and 2030).[20] And there are signs of success to build on: between 1997 and 2015, the share of total GVA from business services in Leeds rose from 8.7 per cent to 15.8 per cent – an increase which took it from below the economy-wide share (9 per cent in 1997) to well above it (12.4 per cent by 2015).[21]

This focus on cities is not a strategy for the few: 69 per cent of the UK population live in cities or their hinterlands, compared to 56 per cent in France and just 40 per cent in Italy.[22] And generating productivity growth in our core cities does not simply support incomes in nearby areas – Buckinghamshire has the same average income as London despite productivity being £20,000 per job lower – it also has the potential to drive further productivity gains in these nearby areas: proximity to large economically productive areas is key in explaining the high levels of productivity in North Hampshire.[23]

But this change will be far from easy or swift. Coming close to halving the productivity gap between London and Manchester (to that seen between Edinburgh and London or Lyon and Paris ie 15 to 20 per cent) requires change equivalent to increasing Manchester's size, graduate share, and capital stocks by 20 per cent. This amounts to many tens of billions of pounds of investment and an increase in Greater Manchester's size by just over 500,000 workers. Change on that scale should be our objective, but it is not consistent with national politicians refusing to concentrate their efforts or local politicians being unable to embrace the disruption involved because they lack the powers to shape it. On both the scale of investment and the crucial role for devolved governance arrangements enabling meaningful economic leadership, there are international lessons to learn from successful 'turn-around' cities.[24]

20 Department for Levelling Up, Housing and Communities, Levelling up the United Kingdom, February 2022.

21 ONS, Regional Gross Value Added (Income Approach) by Local Authority in the UK.

22 Analysis of OECD, Metropolitan Areas Dataset.

23 P Brandily et al., Bridging the gap: What would it take to narrow the UK's productivity disparities, Resolution Foundation, June 2022.

24 P Collier et al., Chapter in Economy 2030 Inquiry international case studies book, Resolution Foundation, forthcoming.

Once again, it is important to consider what this strategy will, and will not, achieve. Successfully closing productivity gaps between cities does not mean every city becoming like London: they will, and would, specialise in different sectors and remain very different in size, culture, and housing costs. But ensuring that more places are part of the cutting edge of the UK economy holds out the possibility of raising national growth and shrinking regional productivity gaps. Although it should raise incomes in poorer regions and reduce national inequality, within-region inequality in productivity and incomes would be likely to widen. Policy makers will need to proactively seek to connect those from more deprived areas to the opportunities created. And without an active housing policy, higher productivity and earnings will lead to higher housing costs, with much of the benefits of economic success flowing to the owners of land rather than workers.[25]

British firms investing more is central to their own, and the country's, future

Many of the challenges the UK is wrestling with have parallels elsewhere: low productivity growth in Italy, high inequality in the US, or an economy dominated by its capital city (France). But when it comes to low business investment, the UK is in a league of its own. This low level of investment may have made sense when the UK was the most advanced economy in the world with a huge capital stock advantage over its competitors, but that was a century ago: the current state of affairs is a recipe for relative decline. In the 40 years to 2019, total fixed investment in the UK averaged 19 per cent of GDP, the lowest in the G7 and some 4 percentage points below G7 average of 23 per cent.[26] Persistent low investment means that virtually all of the productivity gap with France is explained by French workers having more capital to work with.[27] It should be obvious that UK policy debates should focus on the danger of too little automation rather than too much.[28]

25 E Moretti, Local Labor Markets, in O Ashenfelter & D Card (eds.), Handbook of Labor Economics, North Holland, 2011.

26 Analysis of OECD data. This is calculated as simple averages of the ratio of total gross fixed capital formation (GFCF) to GDP, in current prices.

27 The productivity gap with the US can be partly explained by poor management practices; just 11 per cent of UK firms are as well-managed as the best quarter of US firms. This is covered in detail in: J Oliveira-Cunha et al., Business time: How ready are UK firms for the decisive decade?, Resolution Foundation, November 2021.

28 S Farrell, UK economy has "too few robots", warn MPs, The Guardian, September 2019.

Low investment is not driven by our industrial structure, and nor is the problem in the 2020s with the public sector: after decades of underinvestment the Government has now increased public sector net investment to its highest sustained levels since the 1970s.[29] It is the private sector where our lack of investment is acute and where a renewed economic strategy should focus (Figure 29).[30]

Figure 29: Business investment has underperformed and is not recovering strongly from the pandemic

Index of real business investment, outturn, and select forecasts (2008 = 100): UK

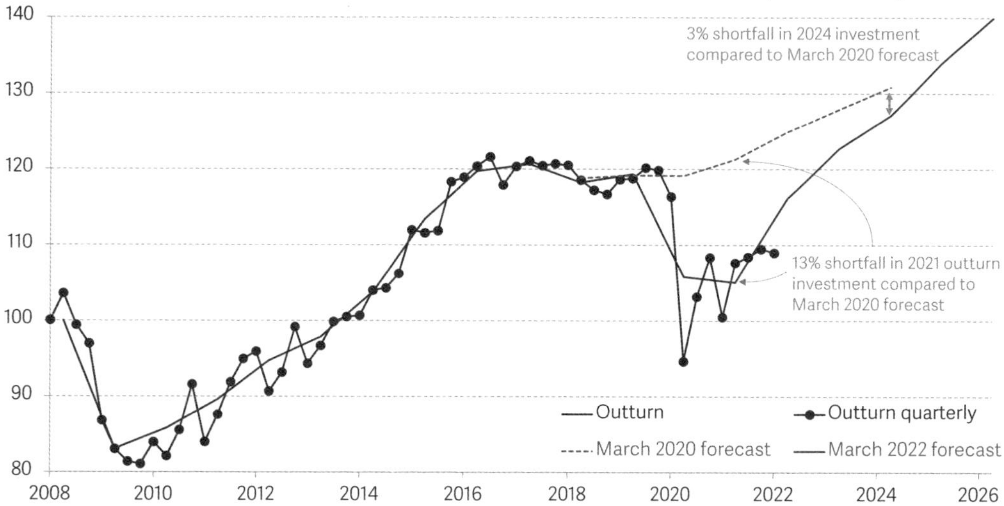

Source: Analysis of OBR, Economic and Fiscal Outlook (various).

A clear economic strategy would in itself help to reduce the economic and policy uncertainty underpinning weak investment growth over the past half-decade. Tax does matter, and the Chancellor has already made a persuasive case for his plans to look again at whether our corporate tax system can do more to encourage capital investment and R&D.[31] But there are limits to the role of traditional tax incentives, which struggle to cover most intangible investment, in an economy like the UK's. Wider questions of business culture, management quality, and financing should be considered, alongside how more firms can benefit from the UK's world-class research.

29 OBR, Public Finance Databank, April 2022.

30 J Leslie, Bouncebackability: The UK corporate sector's recovery from Covid-19, Resolution Foundation, June 2022.

31 R Sunak, Chancellor Rishi Sunak's Mais Lecture 2022, HM Treasury, February 2022.

And once again, the trade offs of a strategy that boosts private sector investment must be recognised. When all potential workers are employed, the amount that the economy can produce is more or less fixed in the short run. Using more workers to make investment goods – such as building materials and machine tools – means having fewer workers available to wait tables. In other words, there is a trade off in the short run between investment and consumption. Alternatively, the investment goods could be imported, rather than made at home with domestic labour, but the extra imports will need to be financed by foreign debt. So, even though higher investment is crucial, we need to recognise that it is not cost free in the short run.

Human capital progress must be sped up and shared out

The immediate post-pandemic period appears to be one where the rising labour force participation we were used to in the 2010s has come to a sharp halt, and as such the quality of labour supply is all the more important.[32] But, as noted in Chapter One, our rate of human capital progress has slowed and the stock is markedly unequal. While popular debates focus on whether we have too much education, the reality is one of growing gaps in education and skills between places, something that the Covid-19 pandemic may have reinforced.[33] Schools in the most deprived areas of England experienced larger real-term spending cuts between 2009-10 and 2019-20 (a 14 per cent reduction) than those in the least deprived areas (a 9 per cent reduction).[34] And debates about whether university expansion has gone too far sit alongside the reality that Higher Education (HE) 'black spots' still exist in the more deprived areas of the UK.[35] Over half of state school-educated young people in London entered HE by age 19, compared to 37 per cent in the South West.[36] Rather than a so-called brain drain from poorer areas, young people from the most-deprived areas

32 M Broome, Big welcomes and long goodbyes: The impact of demographic change in the 2020s, Resolution Foundation, June 2022.

33 L Elliot Major, A Eyles, & S Machin, Pupils lost a third of their expected learning during COVID, with Wales and Scotland even further behind, London School of Economics, July 2021.

34 L Sibieta, 2020 annual report on education spending in England: schools, Institute for Fiscal Studies, September 2020.

35 This inequality is all the more concerning because there is so little education provision between Level 3 (e.g. A-levels) and Level 6 (e.g. degrees). In England, only 4 per cent of 25-year-olds hold a Level 4 or Level 5 qualification as their highest Level. By contrast, in Germany, Levels 4 and 5 make up 20 per cent of all HE enrolments. For more discussion of this see: Department for Education, Independent panel report to the Review of Post-18 Education and Funding, May 2019.

36 Office for Students, Place matters: Inequality, employment and the role of higher education, November 2021.

are 2.5 times less likely to leave their home area upon reaching adulthood than their peers in the least deprived quintile (17 per cent compared to 42 per cent).[37]

Too often, discussions of how to restart this progress get bogged down in a row between the merits of HE and, chronically underfunded, further education (FE) when the evidence shows that they are complementary. HE is key to providing lots of vocational training, such as for nursing, just as FE is both a route into HE and an independent route to many qualifications that are in short supply – from lorry driving to plumbing. The sheer scale of the decline of workplace training in the UK (see Chapter One) needs more attention than employers' complaints about skills shortages.

Significant policy change is already underway in this area. With the Apprenticeship Levy, whatever its wider challenges, the Government is rightly recognising that levies will have to play a central role in turning around the collapse in workplace training. But a purposeful human capital strategy must go much further, recognising the urgency of ensuring we are prepared for the specific challenge of the net zero transition and the general challenge of boosting the UK's competitiveness against the backdrop of stagnant productivity growth.

Barriers to workers' resilience and a more dynamic economy must be addressed

Chapter Two described how the decade ahead will see an acceleration of labour market change, even if not to the highs of previous decades. We must do a better job than we have in the past to help workers losing their jobs navigate this involuntary change. But an economic strategy for the 2020s also needs to go further and confront the worrying lack of 'good change' seen in the UK in recent years.

On both fronts, the UK's lack of income insurance is a concern, limiting risk taking in the labour market, and causing people to suffer unnecessarily when they experience the pain of redundancy (see Figure 30). Our social security system is highly unusual in providing some groups with very little support if they lose their jobs. In the UK, 40 per cent of employed people experience a large loss of income when becoming non-employed, compared to 30 per cent

37 L Judge & D Tomlinson, All over the place: Perspectives on local economic prosperity, The Resolution Foundation, June 2022.

of employed people in Germany and 26 per cent of employed people in France (Figure 30). Such large income shocks make the risk of job loss very high unless wider support is available from family, friends, or savings. It was for good reason that a furlough scheme providing furloughed workers with 80 per cent of their previous earnings was introduced at the start of the pandemic.

Figure 30: The UK has a high proportion of people likely to face a large income loss when becoming unemployed but a low risk of unemployment

Proportion of employed people experiencing a large income loss when becoming non-employed: selected OECD countries, early 2010s or latest

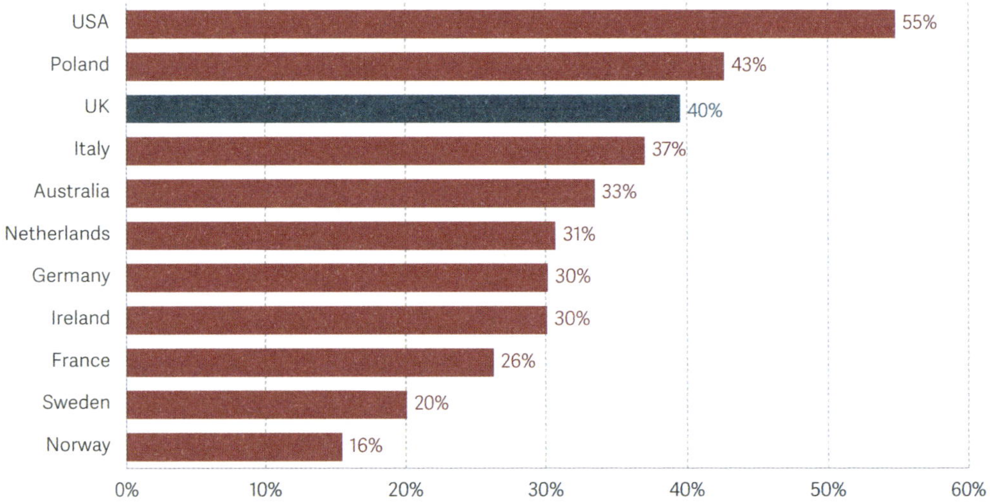

Notes: Large income losses are defined as 20 per cent or more income losses from one year to the next. Data for the United States refer to bi-annual transitions. Data is for the working-age population (18-65).
Source: OECD, A Broken Social Elevator? How to Promote Social Mobility.

Income falls at job loss are larger for middle and higher earners and our qualitative research found that this lack of insurance weighed on their minds when it came to considering taking labour market risks.

> *"I'm the main earner of the house. ... If I really wasn't happy, OK, I might look for other jobs, but I wouldn't just quit mine and walk. If my wife really wasn't happy in her job, we could probably get by without her working while she was looking for something else. But as [the] main breadwinner, no, I see it as my job to keep my salary coming in."*
>
> (Focus group participant, Chippenham)

High, and highly variable, housing costs present another barrier to workers taking up new opportunities. The propensity of young private renters to move home and job fell by two-thirds between 1997 and 2018.[38] In part, this is a result of improved labour markets in previously low-employment areas. But it also reflects private rents rising faster in higher-paying areas, materially reducing or removing the financial incentive to move to more productive places. Even among home owners, large gaps in house prices present a huge barrier to moving into a more expensive area. It is unsurprising, then, that this century a larger proportion of those changing address are relocating to lower-housing-cost areas.[39]

Addressing these barriers to voluntary job moves would benefit individuals, with job switches a key route to higher pay and better job matching.[40] More workers changing jobs and moving into higher-productivity firms would also help with our national productivity challenge, and would be much more useful than boosting the 'long tail' of low-productivity firms that has been a focus for policy makers.[41] Firms in the 'long tail' are so unproductive that they cannot play a major role in raising aggregate output: raising the productivity of the least productive firms employing 40 per cent of workers by 10 per cent would raise productivity by only 1.2 per cent. In contrast, transferring one-tenth of those workers into high-productivity firms (assuming, for illustrative purposes, that could be done without affecting the productivity of those firms) would boost productivity by some 6 per cent.[42]

---

38 L Judge, Moving matters: Housing costs and labour market mobility, Resolution Foundation, June 2019.

39 L Judge, Moving Matters: Housing costs and labour market mobility, Resolution Foundation, June 2019.

40 N Cominetti et al, Changing jobs?: Change in the UK labour market and the role of worker mobility, Resolution Foundation, January 2022.

41 Department for Business, Energy and Industrial Strategy, Business productivity review: call for evidence, May 2018.

42 J Oliveira-Cunha et al., Business time: How ready are UK firms for the decisive decade?, Resolution Foundation, November 2021.

A serious economic strategy will be as hard-headed about lower inequality as it is about higher growth

A renewed economic strategy needs to be as hard-headed about what it will take to ensure a fairer country as what is needed to end its relative economic decline. The goal for the 2020s is not to become like the US, which is far richer than the UK but also far more unequal.

Large gaps between people and places undermine parity of dignity and respect, which are central components of a shared citizenship of a country. As a result, in the long run an unbalanced and unequal economy risks being democratically – and therefore in time economically – unsustainable. Indeed, the last decade across advanced economies has put the nature of the feedback loop from economic dissatisfaction to political upheaval back to deteriorating economic outcomes up in lights.

Figure 31: Place, income, and wealth inequalities are viewed as the most serious divides by Britons

Responses to the question: which three or four of the following types of inequality, if any, do you are most serious in Britain: Great Britain, 2020

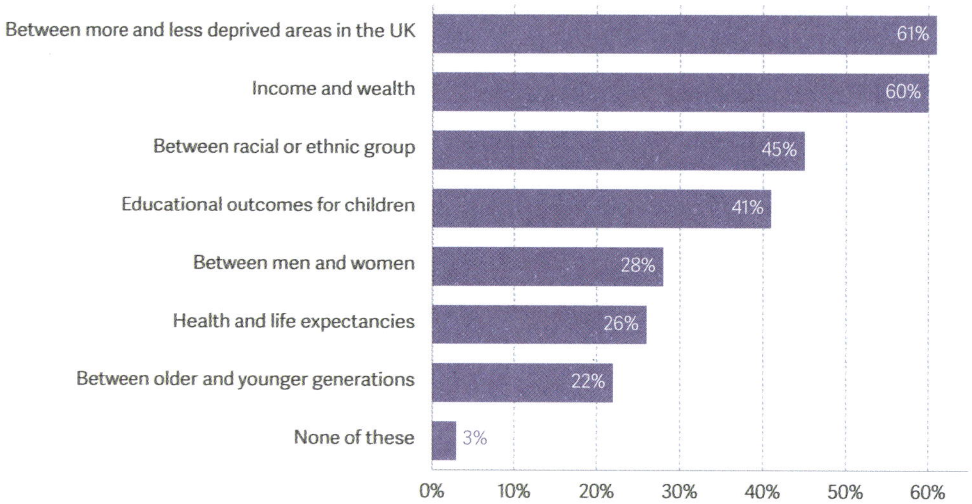

Source: B Duffy et al., Unequal Britain: Attitudes to inequalities after Covid-19, The Policy Institute, King's College London, February 2021.

Democratic legitimacy depends on governments making headway with the challenges that the public pose, and it is clear that people think that inequality between places, and the income and wealth gaps between households, are of concern. As Figure 31 shows, these are raised as the "most serious" inequalities in the country by six in ten Britons.

The gaps between people are not just unsustainable in theory but also in practice. A country where four-tenths of the lowest-income households could not manage for one month on savings pre-pandemic is not resilient.[43] And it is not a sustainable state of affairs that the number of families experiencing destitution at some point in 2019 reached more than 1 million in the UK, an increase of a third compared to 2017.[44]

Too much of our public debate is superficial about what it takes to reduce entrenched inequalities between people and places. Huge productivity gaps between places are supposed to be solved by asking councils to bid for small pots of cash, while political competition on the level of the minimum wage has not be matched by any wider progress on the quality of work for low earners. Firms think that embracing Environmental, Social and Governance (ESG) metrics counts as sufficient progress, while others suggest that a bit more tax and spend might just do the job. A more serious approach would start from the fact that while jobs delivering services exports will be concentrated in certain areas, good jobs and places to live should not be.

Good jobs should be an explicit goal of economic policy

Good jobs, with decent pay and conditions, are the bedrock of widely-shared prosperity and should be the norm everywhere. This not a by-product of a successful economic strategy but a central objective for it. Work is an important source of meaning and contribution for people, as well as a source of income.[45]

43 Analysis of Wealth and Assets Survey.

44 S Fitzpatrick et al., Destitution in the UK 2020, Joseph Rowntree Foundation, December 2020.

45 K Handscomb, L Judge & H Slaughter, Listen up: Individual experiences of work, consumption and society, Resolution Foundation, May 2022.

Britain's flexible labour market is highly effective at generating a good quantity of work. The importance of this for low-income families is often unrecognised: the poorest half of households experienced two-thirds of the jobs growth in the decade after the financial crisis.[46]

However, recognition of the strengths of our flexible labour market – including the way in which the UK has avoided an entrenched insider–outsider problem that can hold back younger or more disadvantaged workers – has too often translated into a reticence to address its weaknesses.[47] The alternative to the status quo is often seen to be a return to the strife of the 1970s.

This false dichotomy has left us relying on a tight labour market, where unemployment is low and vacancies are high, to give workers power to demand better terms and conditions. While attention right now is on workers attempting to exercise such power in the face of high inflation, the lesson from recent decades as a whole is that waiting for a booming labour market to drive up standards is risky. Not only is it far from the norm, but this approach has left us with a labour market with high weekly wage inequality, where individuals do not feel empowered to ask for pay rises,[48] while low-paid workers feel less involved in workplace decisions[49] and face much higher insecurity than the rest of the workforce (see Figure 32).[50] Trade union membership has fallen from over 50 per cent to under 25 per cent during the past four decades,[51] and it is under 10 per cent among the lowest earners in the private sector, with this decline explaining one-sixth of wage inequality among men between 1983 and 2019.[52]

---

46 S Clarke & N Cominetti, Setting the record straight: How record employment has changed the UK, Resolution Foundation, January 2019.

47 T Biergert, Labor market institutions, the insider/outsider divide and social inequalities in employment in affluent countries, Socio-Economic Review, November 2017.

48 Ipsos, Global perceptions of inflation 2022, May 2022.

49 K Shah & D Tomlinson, Work experiences: Changes in the subjective experience of work, Resolution Foundation, September 2021.

50 N Cominetti et al., Low Pay Britain 2022: Low pay and insecurity in the UK labour market, Resolution Foundation, May 2022.

51 U Altunbuken et al., Power plays: The balance of employer and worker power in the UK labour market, Resolution Foundation, July 2022.

52 Analysis of ONS, Labour Force Survey.

Figure 32: Low-paid workers are around three times more likely than higher-paid workers to experience contract insecurity or volatile hours and pay – and the gap has been growing

Proportion of employees experiencing different forms of contract insecurity or volatile hours and pay, by whether in low hourly pay: UK

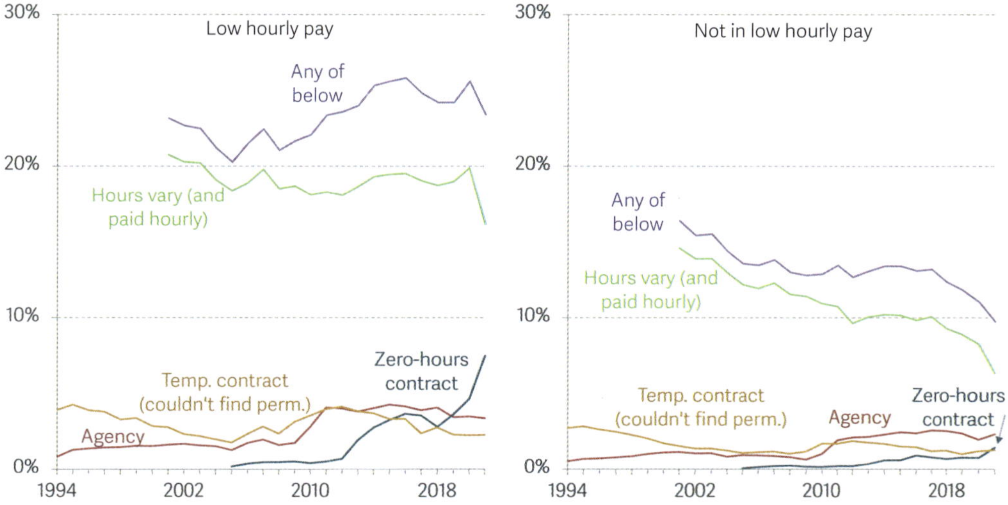

Notes: Low pay is defined as hourly pay below two-thirds of the median. Includes employees only.
Source: Analysis of ONS, LFS.

Two lessons from history should make us consider a more active approach. First, raising the minimum wage from 46 per cent of median pay for those aged 25+ in 1999 towards a goal of two-thirds by 2024, without costing jobs, has provided us with important evidence that power imbalances in the UK labour market exist and that policy can address them.[53] Indeed, the latest evidence suggests that wages could be between 15 and 25 per cent lower than they would otherwise be because of employer power over workers.[54] These

53 Low Pay Commission, The National Living Wage Review (2015-2020), May 2022.

54 Some indirect estimates based upon how quickly workers leave firms with low wages in the US – a labour market with a lower (and falling) labour share, a lower minimum wage, and less collective bargaining than the UK – suggest that wages could be between 15 and 20 per cent lower than they would be otherwise because of employer power over workers. See: M Langella & A Manning, Marshall Lecture 2020: The Measure of Monopsony, Journal of the European Economic Association 19(6), December 2021. Recent evidence from the UK suggests an even higher wage markdown, of between 20 and 25 per cent. See: N Datta, Local Monopsony Power, January 2022.

estimates are extremely imprecise – but a wage markdown of 15 per cent, at the conservative end of these estimates, would mean the average worker today is losing out on almost £100 a week.[55]

Second, low levels of worker power are not an essential feature of our labour market. While other aspects of our economic model have remained largely consistent over decades, our labour market institutions changed markedly during the 1980s.[56]

A new approach might see national labour market regulations used to tackle well-established problems such as low weekly earnings, uncertainties around hours and shifts, and the rise in low-paid self-employment.[57] For example, half of shift workers in Britain receive less than a week's notice of their working hours or schedules.[58] Existing rights also require stronger enforcement, while the UK could also learn from the experiments and institutional reforms taking place in other countries with flexible labour markets to improve labour market outcomes.[59] For example, new sectoral wage boards in New Zealand will set minimum standards across particular sectors of the economy.[60] We should also be thinking about how we might improve the quality of specific occupations that are likely to grow and have the potential to provide large numbers of geographically distributed jobs. There are several over which government has significant influence. Primary examples include health and care work, and the jobs required to install insulation and low-carbon heating in homes across the country.

---

55 U Altunbuken et al., Power plays: The balance of employer and worker power in the UK labour market, Resolution Foundation, July 2022. Average weekly pay (excluding bonuses and arrears) was £562 in April 2022. If employers are marking down pay by 15 per cent, average weekly earnings would be £661 in the absence of employer power over workers – that is, average wages would be £99 a week higher. Source: Office for National Statistics, AWE: Whole Economy Level (£): Seasonally Adjusted Regular Pay Excluding Arrears, June 2022.

56 U Altunbuken et al., Power plays: The balance of employer and worker power in the UK labour market, Resolution Foundation, July 2022.

57 A quarter of employees are in low weekly pay, and 20 per cent of this group (1.4 million people) express a desire to work more hours. For more detail on the range of issues facing low-paid workers in Britain's labour market, see: N Cominetti et al., Low Pay Britain 2022: Low pay and insecurity in the UK labour market, Resolution Foundation, May 2022.

58 J Richardson, The insecurity complex: Low paid workers and the growth of insecure work, Living Wage Foundation, July 2021.

59 Issues with the UK's labour market enforcement regime were explored by the Government-commissioned Taylor Review. Department for Business, Energy and Industrial Strategy, Good work: The Taylor Review of modern working practices, July 2017; for discussion of low-paid self-employment, see: C D'Arcy, The minimum required? Minimum wages and the self-employed, Resolution Foundation, July 2017.

60 D Tomlinson, More than we bargain for: Learning from new debates on how institutions can improve worker pay and security in Anglo-Saxon economies, Resolution Foundation, November 2019.

There are real trade offs of raising wages, particularly in non-tradable jobs such as hospitality, retail, and care. Higher prices are a likely result. But cross-country evidence indicates that, for a given level of productivity, higher wages in non-tradable industries, paid for by higher prices, can make an economy more equal.[61] This reflects workers in non-tradable industries tending to be lower paid. This approach is also consistent with a growth strategy that seeks to raise productivity via workers exiting lower-productivity firms, which is – for example – what was seen after the introduction of the German minimum wage.[62]

Our qualitative research indicates that people understand there is no route to politicians delivering on their promises that all jobs will be available everywhere. Indeed, many feel it would be undesirable in failing to reflect local differences, and are more positive about young people who want to leave their local area for work and study than is commonly portrayed.[63] But realism about what economic activity will take place locally – be that roles in warehouses in Barnsley or tourism in Scarborough – was combined with a clear wish for those jobs to be better. Meeting that wish should be a priority during the 2020s.

> *"[Participant 1] You know, we are not a big city. We're a small coastal town...So, you know, we've got to make the best of what we've got.*
>
> *[Participant 2] If we had a massive water sports centre here too – surfing, windsurfing, powerboating, training for the fishermen as well – that would be a massive help...we're near the coast, it's such a great opportunity that not all have."*
>
> (Focus group participants, Scarborough)

61 We obtain this result by quantifying the relationship across countries and over time between how expensive the cost of a given basket of goods is (i.e. how high the real exchange rate is) and how big the difference is between wages at the 10th and 50th percentiles of the wage distribution, using a linear regression. If the price of tradable goods is similar across countries (because they are tradable) then the real exchange rate will be driven by differences in the price of non-tradable goods. We establish this relationship using a panel linear regression. We control for productivity (TFP) to strip out any effect from richer countries tending to be more or less equal, and because more productive countries tend to be more expensive (the Balassa-Samuelson effect). A 10 per cent increase in the real exchange rate reduces inequality by about 1/6th of a standard deviation. The effect is qualitatively similar for the ratio of the 90th percentile of workers' earnings to the 50th percentile.

62 C Dustmann et al., Reallocation effects of the minimum wage, CReAM discussion paper, February 2020.

63 L Judge & D Tomlinson, All over the place: Perspectives on local economic prosperity, Resolution Foundation, June 2022.

> *"I think it's changed a lot, Barnsley. Every family and generations going back were mining, and that's now shut down. Barnsley is now trying to create industrial estates, putting small technology firms, small businesses, that's cropping up all the way and we've got big warehouses because we're near the M1 motorway. Barnsley is diversifying."*
>
> (Focus group participant, Barnsley)

The public are serious about good places to live

As well as their work, people care deeply about their locality: two-thirds of people in England report that they feel they belong either "very" or "fairly" strongly to their local neighbourhood.[64] Although they are generally very positive about the place they choose to call home, people are also clear about what needs to be done to improve things locally. Issues that are raised almost everywhere should be centre stage in an economic strategy, such as the state of high streets and town centres, the quality and availability of public services, the capacity of local government to deliver the basics, and the challenge of connectivity within and between places.[65]

> *"There isn't really anything...Nothing vintage or nothing cool that's going to make you want to hang out in the town. When I walk through the town I just want to get through it as quickly as possible."*
>
> (Focus group participant, Scarborough)

The Government has received criticism for their 'Levelling Up' agenda focusing on liveability rather than just productivity, but such an approach has merit given the public's reasonable aspirations for their areas that will require economic policy support to realise.[66] But while the direction of travel is positive, the policy approach taken to date – allocating small pots of cash for improving local areas via competitive bidding regimes – is deeply flawed. A striking 18 per cent of all revenue grants and 30 per cent of all capital grants for

64 Department for Digital, Culture, Media & Sport, Community Life Survey 2020/21, July 2021.

65 L Judge & D Tomlinson, All over the place: Perspectives on local economic prosperity, Resolution Foundation, June 2022.

66 Department for Levelling Up, Housing and Communities, Levelling up the United Kingdom, February 2022.

local authorities are wound up every year, making long-term planning difficult.[67] And providing grants for specific improvements misses the importance of the 'basics' that are too often lacking, unsurprisingly with council revenues per person falling by 30 per cent between 2009 and 2019 in the most-deprived places, compared to 15 per cent in the least-deprived places.[68] From long waits at A&E, to teacher shortages and the decaying of our public spaces and high streets – the sense that public services and the public realm are lacking the investment they need is real and acute in poorer areas. This directly feeds through into a sense of local decline in many places, with the proportion of people thinking their local area has deteriorated in the preceding two years rising steadily from 20 per cent in 2013-14 to 26 per cent in 2019-20.[69]

There will be tensions between the push towards fiscal devolution to underpin more local economic leadership discussed above with the need set out here to ensure poorer areas have the funding required for a decent public realm. But it is a tension many other less centralised countries navigate successfully and so should the UK.

Realism about the different roles of different places in our economy should be combined with an ambition to reject the wide gaps in status and quality of life that are too often associated with that. Good jobs and places to live everywhere should be the universalist promise of a renewed economic strategy.

The state will grow, but it must be funded fairly and efficiently

Despite, or perhaps because of, its centrality to politics and policy debates, there is more wishful thinking about the state than any other component of economic strategy. Politicians declare their low-tax 'instincts' while raising taxes to their highest levels since the 1940s, or call for a smaller state and a bigger army.

Forecasts of changes in public spending into the medium-term are heavily dependent on demographic projections, which are revised regularly and often substantially. There are some clear pressures on the size of the state

---

67 A Breach & S Bridgett, Centralisation Nation: How a broken system of local government harms the British economy, Resolution Foundation & Centre for Cities, July 2022.

68 T Harris, L Hodge & D Phillips, English local government funding: Trends and challenges in 2019 and beyond, Institute for Fiscal Studies, November 2019.

69 Department for Digital, Culture, Media & Sport, Community Life Survey 2020/21, July 2021.

in the years ahead: spending on the State Pension will rise as the number of people aged 65 and above increases by 20 per cent between 2020 and 2030; [70] healthcare spending has been growing faster than other spending throughout the 2010s and this is likely to continue;[71] and net zero will require the state to do more. In addition, pressures to address new geopolitical realities (with new commitments to raise defence spending to 2.5 per cent of GDP) and to reverse the deterioration in the quality of public services will persist.[72] On the other side of the ledger, the latest population forecasts imply a large (9 per cent) fall in the number of under-15s over the course of the 2020s, reducing pressures on education spending;[73] and recent revisions to population projections assume a lower life expectancy than the previous vintage and a lower 'old age dependency ratio'.[74]

So a serious economic strategy needs to wrestle with how to manage fiscal pressures, in whatever shape and size they materialise, at a time when many of the strategies used to respond to previous spending pressures are either not available or desirable. Health, education, and social security spending nearly doubled as a proportion of GDP between 1955-56 and 2019-20, in large part funded by shrinking defence spending (from 8 per cent of GDP in 1955-6 to 2 per cent – the level committed to as part of NATO membership – in 2022) or cutting public sector investment (a damaging trend that the Government has rightly reversed).

With other margins of adjustment exhausted, taxes are rising: the latest forecasts are for them to hit levels not seen since the Second World War (or the 1980s, depending on the measure focused on). The question of who pays these taxes (across the income distribution and the generations) and on what basis (be it income, expenditure or wealth) will be central. And new answers will be needed. Over recent decades, both main parties have turned to increases in National Insurance (NI) to fund spending increases. Most recently, in September 2021, the Government announced additional spending on health and social care, funded by increases in NI worth around £17 billion per year.[75]

---

70 M Broome, Big welcomes and long goodbyes: The impact of demographic change in the 2020s, Resolution Foundation, June 2022.

71 K Shah, J Smith & D Tomlinson, Under pressure: Managing fiscal pressures in the 2020s, Resolution Foundation, February 2022.

72 J Lee, UK defence spending to rise as dangers increase - PM , BBC, June 2022.

73 C Giles & S Joiner, Population changes provide UK with unexpected boost to public finances, Financial Times, February 2022.

74 ONS, National population projections: 2020-based interim, January 2022.

75 OBR, Economic and Fiscal Outlook, March 2022.

These tax rises are progressive, but fall disproportionately on the working-age population: a typical 25-year-old today will pay an extra £12,600 over their working lives from the employee part of the tax rise alone, compared to nothing for landlords and most pensioners.[76] Landlords are not asked to contribute, while their working tenants very much are. This is not what a good strategic response to the dilemma of needing to fund higher spending in an era of weak earnings growth looks like.

Figure 33: Income from diverse sources is liable for less tax

Total amount of tax-free income available to a person with earnings and/or pension income only, and a person using every available relief: UK, July 2022 to March 2023

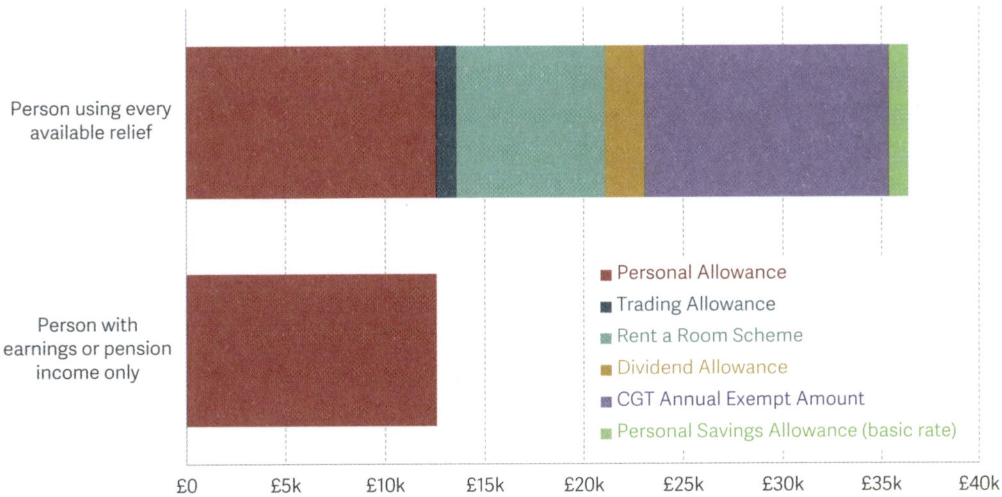

Notes: Person using every available relief includes: income from employment, self-employment, room-rental, dividends, capital gains & savings. A person could also use the tax free ISA allowance on top of this, however all ISA income is tax-free so this has not been included here.
Source: Analysis of HMRC.

Fairer, and more efficient, approaches will need to be explored in the years ahead. Our tax system currently hugely benefits those (largely richer and older) who do not rely solely on wages for their income and who often have choices over which form to take it in. Not only do many of them incur a lower tax rate than is charged on earnings (for example, capital gains are

76 T Bell et al, Nationally Insured?: New taxes and new spending to address key Department for Health and Social Care priorities, Resolution Foundation September 2021.

taxed at lower rates than other income), but – as demonstrated in Figure 33 – those with multiple sources of income (from the likes of dividends, capital gains, rent, or savings) can exploit separate tax allowances to pay far lower tax than an employee with the same income. [77]

Policy makers will also need to wrestle with the related challenge of the very different trajectories for income and wealth discussed in Chapter One. Although the amount of wealth held by private households has risen from three times GDP to nearly eight times GDP since the 1980s, there has been no increase in the related tax take as a proportion of GDP, as Figure 34 shows. [78]

Figure 34: Wealth tax revenues have not risen in line with wealth

Total wealth and wealth taxes as a proportion of GDP: GB, 1965-2020

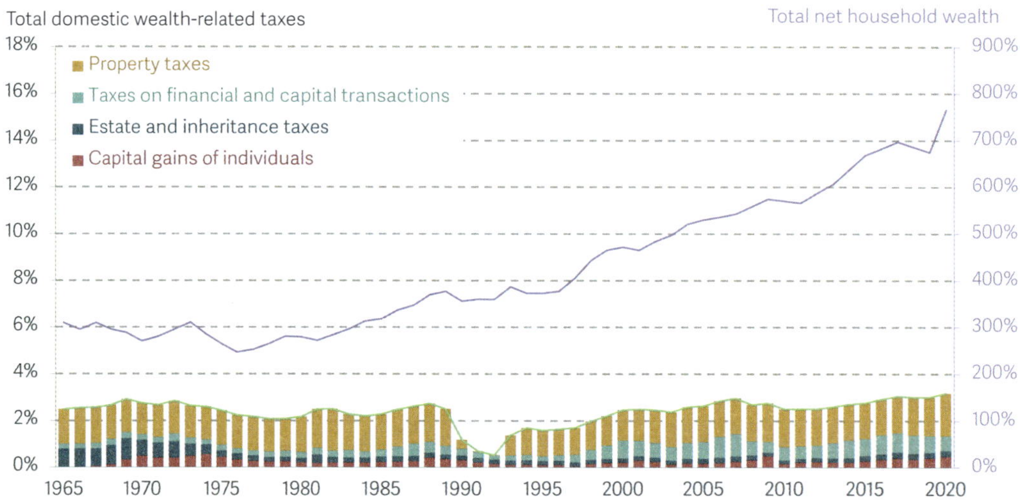

Notes: Estimated 2020 value calculated by multiplying the value of wealth as a proportion of GDP from the Wealth and Asset Survey by the growth rate in this value found between 2019 and 2020 in the National Accounts.
Source: Analysis of D Blake & J Orszag, 'Annual estimates of personal wealth holdings in the United Kingdom since 1948', Applied Financial Economics 9, 1999; ONS, UK National Accounts, ONS, Total Wealth, Wealth in Great Britain, ONS Gross Domestic Product at market prices; Current price: Seasonally adjusted £m; OECD, Details of Tax Revenue.

77 G Bangham et al., Unhealthy finances: How to support the economy today and repair the public finances tomorrow, Resolution Foundation, November 2021.

78 K Shah, Wealth on the eve of a crisis: Exploring the UK's pre-pandemic wealth distribution, Resolution Foundation, January 2022.

Those on lower incomes must be protected from the costs of net zero and a benefits system that leaves many exposed to hardship

While fair taxes are often at the centre of political debates, the fair financing of the net zero transition will be a relatively new addition during the 2020s. But it will be a crucial one if the high levels of public support for net zero, and progress on the transition itself, are to be maintained. The state's top priority should be to protect low-income households from the upfront costs, in particular when it comes to the home heating transition, where the most immediate challenge is improving the energy efficiency of our housing stock. After years of policy failures, efficiency installations in Britain's homes are running at around 10 per cent of the levels seen in the early 2010s.[79] To keep us on track for net zero this needs to change fast, with low-income property owners highly exposed: 72 per cent of them live in homes rated EPC band D (the average energy efficiency rating for UK homes) or below.[80] The average cost for bringing such homes up to band C standard is estimated at over £8,000 per household, which means it simply will not happen without government intervention given that the average income of poorer homeowners after housing costs is around £9,100.

The challenge to some lower-income households posed by the transition to net zero sits alongside a longer-term trend: the incomes of the poorest in society are low and have failed to keep pace with the rest of society in recent years. Living standards have barely improved for lower-income households for much of this century: the typical incomes of the poorest fifth of the population were no higher on the eve of the pandemic than they were back in 2004-05, despite GDP per person growing by 12 per cent over this period. This partly reflects decisions around benefit levels, as we show in Figure 35: the basic level of unemployment benefit has been completely decoupled from income levels of the rest of society and now stands at its lowest rate on record (£77 per week, which is equivalent to just 13 per cent of average pay).[81]

---

79 A Corlett & J Marshall, Shrinking footprints: The impacts of the net zero transition on households and consumption, Resolution Foundation, May 2022.

80 Properties are rated on how efficient a property is, with bands from A to G. The most efficient homes are in band A, and the least efficient are in band G. The Government has set a target of all homes reaching a C rating on the EPC scale by 2035.

81 A Corlett, F Odamtten & L Try, The Living Standards Audit 2022, Resolution Foundation, July 2022.

Figure 35: The basic level of unemployment benefit is now just 13 per cent of average pay, its lowest level on record

Value of selected benefits as a share of Average Weekly Earnings: UK

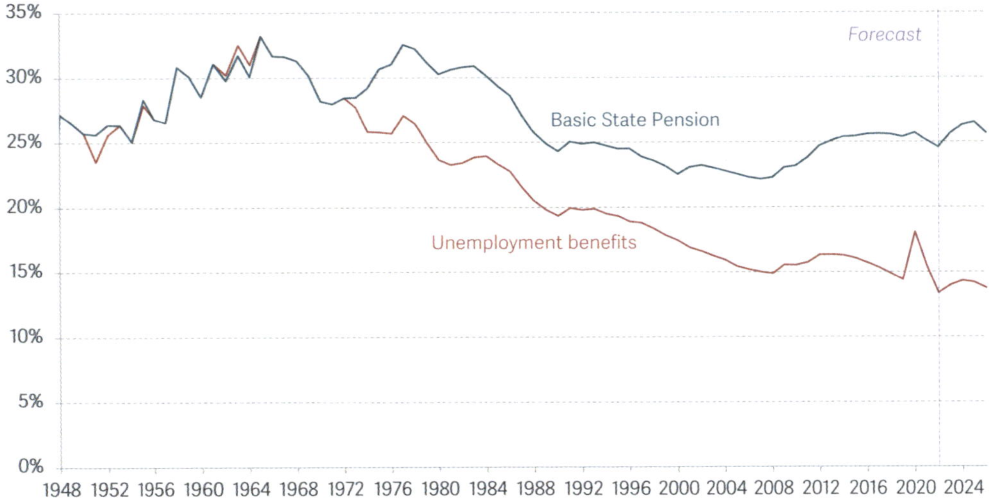

Source: Analysis of DWP, Abstract of Benefit Statistics; ONS, CPI; OBR, Economic and Fiscal Outlook March 2022; Bank of England, Monetary Policy Report May 2022.

Developments for disabled people and larger families are particularly concerning. While the overall spend on disability and ill-health related benefits has increased because of a rising caseload, the generosity of those benefits has not. In fact, disabled people are at increased risk of poverty, with almost a third (31 per cent) of households with a disabled adult being in poverty in 2019-20, compared to 19 per cent of families in which no one is disabled.[82] Similarly, the result of successive social security policy changes, such as the introduction of the benefit cap and two-child limit, is that by 2019-20, almost half (47 per cent) of families with three or more children were in poverty, up from 33 per cent in 2012-13.[83] An renewed economic strategy that is even remotely serious about reducing inequality will need to put these trends into reverse.

82 Joseph Rowntree Foundation, UK Poverty 2022: The essential guide to understanding poverty in the UK, January 2022.

83 M Brewer et al., Social insecurity: Assessing trends in social security to prepare for the decade of change ahead, The Resolution Foundation, January 2022.

Our macroeconomic policy framework needs rebooting

Spending pressures will be easier to meet if we can sustain GDP growth, while avoiding major downturns is particularly important for those on lower incomes. For example, after the 1980s recession those towards the bottom of the income distribution were six times more likely to be unemployed than those towards the top.[84] These are among the reasons why a strong macroeconomic policy framework, where policy makers have the tools to stabilise the economy, is crucial.

Today's macroeconomic policy framework – centred around an inflation-targeting Bank of England that has the primary responsibility for stabilising the economy – faces significant challenges. The focus today is on high inflation, but the Bank clearly has the tools to avoid that becoming entrenched and is using them, with interest rates increasing by 1.15 percentage points between December 2021 and June 2022 to reach the highest level in 13 years.[85] But the Bank has less room for manoeuvre when it comes to the opposite problem, a downturn. With interest rates trending down now for several decades, the central bank has far less scope to cut them to support the economy during a recession because of the zero effective lower bound (ELB) on interest rates (which means they cannot fall materially below zero).

Just because this is not today's problem does not mean it is one we should continue to ignore. Macroeconomic policy makers have had to improvise in the last two recessions. When the financial crisis hit, they partially relaxed the ELB with quantitative easing (pushing down longer-term interest rates) and a discretionary fiscal stimulus. The same thing happened again in the Covid-19 recession, albeit with fiscal policy doing the lion's share of the work.

But after 14 years and two 'once in a generation' recessions with Bank rate at or near the ELB, there is a strong case for more sustainably reforming the macroeconomic policy framework for the new era we find ourselves in. The scale of constraint in the current system is illustrated by the fact that interest rates were cut by just 0.65 per cent in the pandemic compared to a norm of around 5 percentage points in a downturn before the financial crisis.[86] If policy does not have enough room to react in the next recession, living standards,

84 J Smith et al., Recession ready? Assessing the UK's macroeconomic framework, Resolution Foundation, September 2019.

85 Bank of England, Bank Rate increased to 1.25% – June 2022: Monetary Policy Summary and minutes of the Monetary Policy Committee meeting, June 2022.

86 J Smith et al., Recession ready? Assessing the UK's macroeconomic framework, Resolution Foundation, September 2019.

especially of low-to-middle income households, will suffer. The dangers of repeated improvisation include a lack of certainty about how policy makers will respond as well as institutional risks from confusion about the respective roles of monetary and fiscal policy (this is well illustrated by recent proposals to tax the banking system, either implicitly[87] or explicitly,[88] in order to mitigate the costs to the taxpayer or rising interest rates).

There are a number of avenues that should be explored to reduce the constraint on monetary policy, including a higher inflation target or moves to make negative interest rates practical in the UK. The way in which fiscal policy is able to help support the economy in a recession could also be strengthened, while recognising that the recent pattern of very large fiscal stimulus during a downturn will require lower borrowing in normal times than would otherwise be the case.

Towards a renewed economic strategy

Despite its huge strengths and privileges, Britain has become a stagnation nation of low growth and high inequality. The task of the 2020s is to turn that around. This will require us to be honest about where growth may come from, and the scale of change required to meaningfully address inequalities between people and places. But this chapter has also demonstrated that policy makers should reject fatalism, given the significant strengths of the UK economy and the existence of plausible routes to rebuilding our economic strategy during the 2020s. This initial outline of a plausibly successful economic strategy for the UK will give direction to our work in the second half of The Economy 2030 Inquiry. From this jumping off point – not bound by the economic or policy status quo, but being realistic about where we start from as a country and some of the legacies that need to be grappled with – we will build a series of proposals that when combined could turn a strategy into a reality.

Implementing it wouldn't be easy, with difficult economic and political trade offs. The scale of those challenges means some will ask whether it is worth it, especially if they see slow growth and our high inequality as inevitable (perhaps because of lower technological progress and increased returns to skills). The next, and final, chapter discusses how we should wrestle with these questions.

87 National Institute of Economic and Social Research, Quantitative tightening: Protecting monetary policy from fiscal encroachment – one year on, June 2022.

88 F Van Lerven & D Caddick, Between a rock and a hard place: The case for a tiered reserve monetary policy framework, New Economics Foundation, June 2022.

Chapter Five

The returns to inclusive growth

Chapter summary

- Renewing the UK's economic strategy will be far from easy, economically or politically. But those questioning whether the gains will be worth it, given slowing growth at the global frontier, ignore the fact that the UK is a long way from that frontier.

- Australia, Canada, France, Germany and the Netherlands are not the richest, or most equal, countries in the world and would long have been considered the UK's peers. But we're now 21 per cent poorer than them on average, dwarfing the Office for Budget Responsibility's forecast of a 4 per cent hit to our long-run productivity from Brexit.

- These countries are also more equal than the UK, such that if we reduced inequality to the levels in the comparison group it would raise incomes for the poorest fifth of the country by more than 20 per cent while reducing them for the richest in society.

- If we were able to close the gap in income and inequality it would have a transformative effect, increasing incomes by over 40 per cent among the poorest fifth of the country, and around one third for the middle, without reducing incomes at the top (indeed, they would still rise slightly).

- This demonstrates the size of the prize available. A better future for the UK does not need global growth to suddenly accelerate, or Britain to match American levels of productivity and Scandinavian levels of inequality. It just requires us to catch up with similar countries who, in the scheme of things, are not so very different to us. There is a lot to play for, especially for those on low-to-middle incomes.

- The next step is to design the policies for us to achieve a richer and fairer Britain. The second phase of The Economy 2030 Inquiry will undertake this detailed work to contribute to debates on how Britain navigates the 2020s.

This book has shown why the UK requires a renewed economic strategy for the 2020s and has begun the task of outlining what a plausible one could look like. It has grappled with some of the constraints, pressures, and trade offs that make developing a new strategy such a difficult task for any government. Given the political and economic challenges involved, some will question how achievable a material increase in growth or reduction in inequality is for a relatively small and mature economy like the UK in the 21st century. Maybe the potential gains from the effort are too small to justify the difficult political choices that it would inevitably entail: perhaps muddling through with the current approach is the best that can be done?

In this final chapter of the book, we consider these arguments and try to give a sense of the potential gains from a return to inclusive growth in the 2020s and beyond. The conclusion is that the cost of stagnation is very high indeed and the plausible prize from ending it is well worth aiming for.

Growth at the productivity frontier may slow, but the UK is not at that frontier

Economic debates about the potential for growth often start from questions of whether developments in technology have slowed, arguing that this means a period of much weaker growth is the best that can be achieved. Developments at the productivity frontier (currently the US) are of course relevant for the UK. If growth for the leader slows, in the long run the potential for growth for the laggards – including the UK – is lower too.[1]

Turning points in growth at the productivity frontier are rare and very difficult to forecast. Some well-informed observers expect US productivity growth to remain slow, consistent with the idea that over the long term it is driven by episodic major innovations, such as steam or electricity, that rarely come along.[2] Others remain optimistic and view the current digital and low-carbon transitions as precisely such an opportunity for widespread productivity gains – for them, the current lull in performance stems from the fact that we are living in the lag between technological advance and widespread adoption (an

1 J Fernald & R Inkaar, The UK productivity 'puzzle' in an international comparative perspective, The Productivity Institute, April 2022.

2 R Gordon, The Rise and Fall of American Growth: The U.S. Standard of Living since the Civil War, Princeton University Press, August 2017; J Fernald & H Li, Is slow still the new normal for GDP growth?, Federal Reserve Bank of San Francisco, June 2019; T Philippon, Additive growth, NBER Working Papers No. 29950, April 2022.

echo of the Solow paradox in the 1980s when the gains from the ICT revolution were yet to show up in statistics).[3]

Crucially, however, the UK's growth prospects over the next few decades need not hinge on which of these views is correct. Even if the potential rate of growth for those at the productivity frontier slows, the gap between the UK and those at the vanguard will still be very large indeed. As discussed in Chapter One, productivity (measured by GDP per hour) in the US, France and Germany is between 15 and 18 per cent higher than in the UK. There is an awful lot of productivity 'catch-up' for us to aim at.

The hit to incomes from Brexit is much smaller than the gap with the frontier

To put the scale of catch-up growth into perspective, consider the single issue that has dominated economic policy discussions over the past six years: Brexit. The UK's withdrawal from the EU has raised the costs of international trade with our largest trading partner. The result, as discussed in Chapter Two, will be a reduction in the levels of productivity and incomes in the UK relative to where they would otherwise have been.

This will act as a significant headwind to growth rates in the years ahead as the UK shifts to a new, poorer, steady state. The OBR estimates that once this state is reached, UK productivity will be 4 per cent lower than if the country had remained in the EU.[4] This headwind is significant and it is right that it is highlighted and debated. But it is just a quarter of the size of the 16 per cent productivity gap with those nations at the productivity frontier: even accounting for any Brexit headwinds, the potential for considerable catch-up growth remains. Just as the country faced entrenched economic challenges before Brexit occurred, there still remains a huge amount of scope for improvement in its wake.

---

3 E Brynjolfsson, D Rock & C Syverson, Artificial intelligence and the modern productivity paradox: A clash of expectations and statistics, NBER Working Papers No. 24001, November 2017.

4 OBR, Brexit analysis, May 2022. According to the OBR, 0.4 per cent of the 4 per cent productivity hit is related to lower EU migration (which is partially compensated for by non-EU migration to the UK). The smaller working population implies that 3.6 per cent of the productivity reduction is equivalent to a fall in GDP per capita. The OBR estimates that two-fifths of the productivity effect had already taken place by January 2021, largely driven by falls in investment due to uncertainty post-referendum.

The UK is a long way from best in class on both prosperity and inequality

The other key dimension of the UK's stagnation is high inequality. As detailed in Chapter One, the gaps between places and households are large in the UK – and larger than in many comparator countries. But just as catching up with the US's productivity levels is a very tall order – Britain was last at the productivity frontier at the start of the 20th century – so too would dragging UK income inequality down to the level of Norway any time soon.[5]

Rather than focus just on the 'leading' countries when it comes to growth and equality, we can instead compare ourselves to a broader range of economies that more closely resemble the UK to gauge what the potential for improvement might be. When we do so, as Figure 36 shows, we see that the UK has average household incomes but relatively high income inequality when compared to similar advanced economies.

Figure 36: Compared to other OECD countries, the UK is relatively unequal with unexceptional average incomes

Gini coefficient and average disposable income per capita at PPP: 2018, OECD

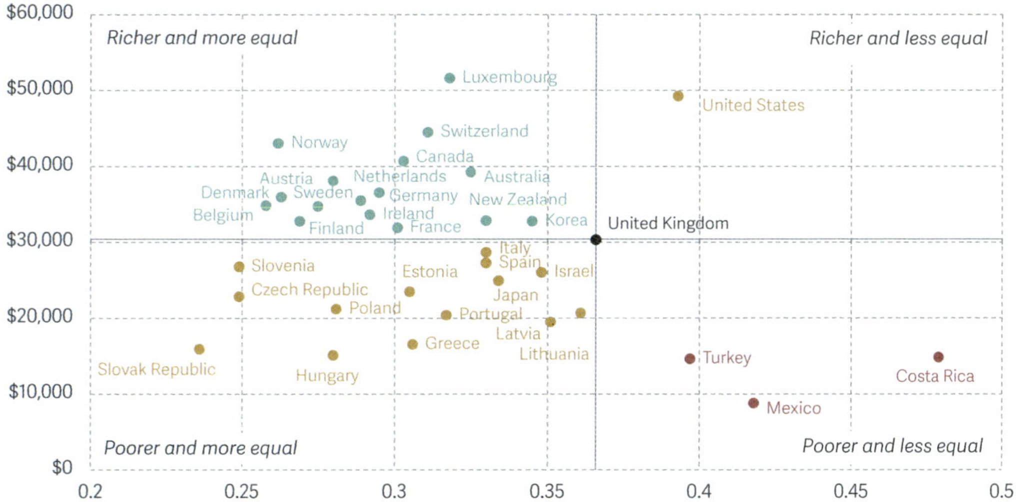

Notes: Income is equivalised.
Source: OECD, Income Inequality Database.

5 A Bergeaud, G Cette & R Lecat, Productivity trends in advanced countries between 1890 and 2012, Review of Income and Wealth, September 2016.

Some countries, such as the US, have higher average incomes but much higher inequality. Others, such as Poland, have the opposite, and others still are very small (e.g. Luxembourg) or have large resource endowments (e.g. Norway), making them unhelpful benchmarks for the UK. However, there are several comparably sized countries with incomes that are both higher on average and more evenly distributed than the UK's – we focus on a set of similar comparator economies: Australia, Canada, France, Germany, and the Netherlands.

Converging towards the frontier would raise incomes for everyone, but especially those on low and middle incomes

The existence of a cluster of other countries with incomes that are both higher and more evenly distributed than the UK's suggests that there could be scope for 'catch-up' on both these fronts – that is, for the UK to move to average incomes and inequality levels more in line with the countries in the top-left of Figure 36.

These gaps with other countries are sufficiently large that success in closing them would make a very material difference to UK living standards, especially for those on low incomes. We do not even have to compare ourselves to the highest-income places (such as the US) or the most equal (such as Norway) to see just how far behind the 'frontier' on both growth and inequality the UK is.

For example, there is a 21 per cent gap between average disposable incomes in the UK and our set of similar comparator economies. What closing this gap might mean for household incomes depends, among other things, on distributional outcomes. Figure 37 helps us think about this. It shows what UK convergence on the levels of inequality and incomes per capita in our comparison group of nations, both separately and together, would do for different types of UK households.[6] Raising average incomes by 21 per cent, holding inequality constant, would have the same effect across the board. And reducing inequality to the levels in the comparison group would, in isolation, raise incomes for the poorest fifth of the country by 20 per cent while reducing them for the richest in society. But combining the two impacts together – that is, closing the gap on growth and inequality – would have huge effects at the bottom and middle of the income distribution, increasing incomes by more than 40 per cent among the poorest fifth of the country, without reducing

6 This analysis extends the international comparisons shown in: A Corlett, F Odamtten & L Try, The Living Standards Audit 2022, Resolution Foundation, July 2022.

incomes at the top (indeed, they would still rise slightly).[7] This distribution of gains – bottom heavy but widely shared – is hardly without precedent. But it is unlikely to occur without a deliberate strategy.

Figure 37: Raising and equalising incomes in line with five similar countries would boost incomes in the lowest quintile by over 40 per cent

Effect on incomes of moving to the average levels of inequality and incomes in Australia, Canada, France, Germany and the Netherlands, by income quintile

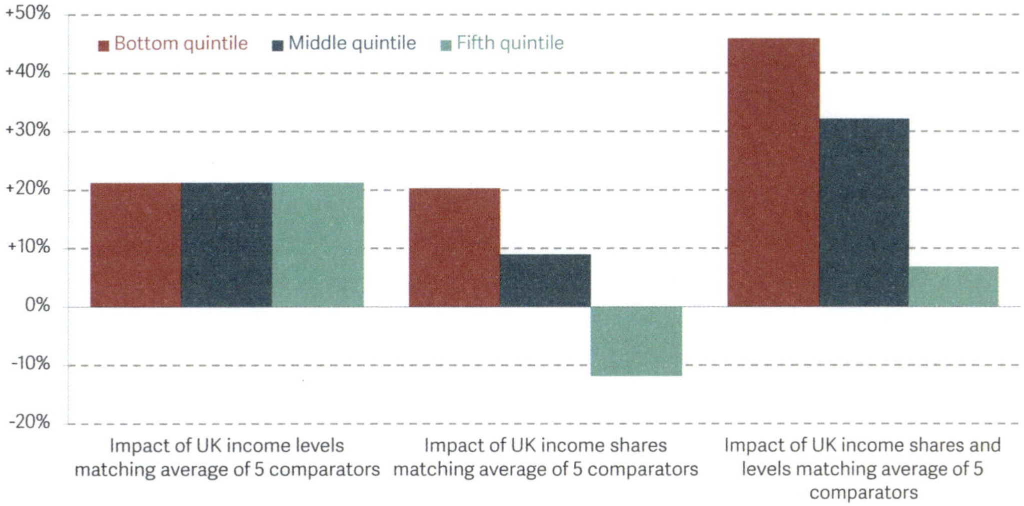

Source: Analysis of OECD, Income Distribution Database.

We are not arguing that this sort of shift is easy to achieve. This is a heavily stylised example – a thought experiment – to illustrate the order of magnitude of the gains that could arise from a sustained improvement in performance on growth and inequality in the decade ahead. It will be the job of the final report in The Economy 2030 Inquiry to advance a policy agenda capable of realising at least some of these potential benefits.

What this illustration brings home is just how much difference it would make to households in Britain if we could get even part of the way towards the levels of prosperity and equality in similar countries, in the same way that Chapter One set out the costs of our recent relative decline. The potential size of the prize is enormous. To put it another way, these figures highlight what

7 The gains for the very lowest income households would be even larger than those shown here, just as the impact of making the UK as equal as the average across comparator economies would have a larger effect on the highest income households. The top 10 per cent of UK households have an income share of 29 per cent, compared to 24 per cent across the five comparator economies.

we are giving up if we continue to stagnate. They should serve to harden our resolve when confronted with the all-too-common suggestion that improved economic and social performance is just too difficult. A better future for the UK does not need global growth to suddenly accelerate, or for Britain to achieve American levels of productivity, never mind become the most equal country on earth. It just requires us to have the resolve to do what is necessary to converge with nearby countries that, in the greater scheme of things, are not so very different to us.

Towards a plausible economic strategy

This book comes at the mid-point of The Economy 2030 Inquiry, bringing together our evidence on the persistent economic problems facing the UK and how recent shocks and transitions – Brexit, Covid-19, and net zero – will play out over the 2020s. It has argued that Britain's fundamental problem (which these changes will mostly compound rather than ameliorate) is economic stagnation characterised by persistent low growth and high inequality. The risks of continuing down the current path for another decade are very real: not just in terms of further relative economic decline and faltering living standards, but also in relation to our capacity to make a success of the transition to a low-carbon future and, ultimately, the stability of our democracy.

The analysis presented here confirms the scale of the challenge but also demonstrates the difference that good policy can make. It provides confidence that the many economic challenges we face – whether longstanding or those coming down the track – are capable of being tackled and that the UK faces them with many strengths. But this will require a reset of our economic strategy. And that, in turn, demands not just a long-term commitment to new policy agendas but also a shift in governing mindset. We need to reject the tendency towards either fatalism or complacency that characterises far too much of the national conversation about Britain's economic future, and replace it with a seriousness of purpose that is all too often lacking.

This book has outlined the contours of an economic strategy that could provide a plausible route out of stagnation. The second half of The Economy 2030 Inquiry will undertake the detailed work of developing this outline into a comprehensive and integrated set of policies and institutional reforms that, taken together, add up to a new economic strategy to help guide Britain through the 2020s and beyond to a richer, fairer, and greener future.

The Commissioners

A small Commission of seven high-profile thinkers and doers provides The Economy 2030 Inquiry's strategic leadership and direction. Its membership is:

Baroness Minouche Shafik
Director of London School of Economics and Political Science

Sir Clive Cowdery
Founder of the Resolution Foundation and chairman of the Resolution Group

Adam Tooze
Kathryn and Shelby Cullom Davis Professor of History, Columbia University

Dani Rodrik
Ford Foundation Professor of International Political Economy at Harvard University

Dame Carolyn Fairbairn
Former Director-General of the Confederation of British Industry

Frances O'Grady
General Secretary of the British Trades Union Congress

Lord Nicholas Stern
I G Patel Chair of Economics and Government, LSE

The Advisory Group

The Economy 2030 Inquiry is also overseen by an Advisory Group, who provide external input, challenge and advice. Its membership is:

Alex Beer, Nuffield Foundation

Alex Brazier, BlackRock

Chiara Criscuolo, OECD

Chris Colvin, Queen's University, Belfast

Darra Singh, EY

Deborah Cadman, Birmingham City Council

Gary Gillespie, Scottish Government

James Benford, HM Treasury

Jane Green, Nuffield College, University of Oxford

Jeromin Zettelmeyer, IMF and PIIE

Kate Bell, TUC

Kelly Beaver, Ipsos MORI

Pat Richie, Metro Dynamics

Rachel Ashworth, Cardiff Business School

Rain Newton-Smith, CBI

Rebecca Heaton, Lloyds Banking Group

Sushil Wadhwani, PGIM Wadhwani

The Economy 2030 Inquiry publications

All publications can be read at economy2030.resolutionfoundation.org.

- The UK's decisive decade: The launch report of The Economy 2030 Inquiry
- Levelling up and down Britain: How the labour market recovery varies across the country
- Work experiences: Changes in the subjective experience of work
- The Carbon Crunch: Turning targets into delivery
- Trading places: Brexit and the path to longer-term improvements in living standards
- Home is where the heat (pump) is: Assessing the Government's Heat and Buildings Strategy
- Business time: How ready are UK firms for the decisive decade?
- Begin again? Assessing the permanent implications of Covid-19 for the UK's labour market
- More trade from a land down under: The significance of trade agreements with Australia and New Zealand
- Social mobility in the time of Covid: Assessing the social mobility implications of Covid-19
- Changing jobs? Change in the UK labour market and the role of worker mobility
- Social Insecurity: Assessing trends in social security to prepare for the decade of change ahead
- A presage to India: Assessing the UK's new Indo-Pacific trade focus
- Under pressure: Managing fiscal pressures in the 2020s

- Under new management: How immigration policy change will, and won't, affect the UK's path to becoming a high-wage, high-productivity economy
- Shrinking footprints: The impacts of the net zero transition on households and consumption
- Enduring strengths: Analysing the UK's current and potential economic strengths, and what they mean for its economic strategy, at the start of the decisive decade
- Listen up: Individual experiences of work, consumption and society
- Growing clean: Identifying and investing in sustainable growth opportunities across the UK
- Low Pay Britain 2022: Low pay and insecurity in the UK labour market
- Bouncebackability: The UK corporate sector's recovery from Covid-19
- All over the place: Perspectives on local economic prosperity
- Right where you left me? Analysis of the Covid-19 pandemic's impact on local economies in the UK
- Big welcomes and long goodbyes: The impact of demographic change in the 2020s
- Net zero jobs: The impact of the transition to net zero on the UK labour market
- The Big Brexit: An assessment of the scale of change to come from Brexit
- Income outcomes: Assessing income gaps between places across the UK
- Bridging the Gap: What would it take to narrow the UK's productivity disparities?
- Power plays: Assessing the impact of, and changes to, worker and firm power in the UK economy
- As good as it gets? The forces driving economic stagnation and what they mean for the decade ahead

The Resolution Foundation

The Resolution Foundation is an independent think-tank focused on improving the living standards of those on low-to-middle incomes. We work across a wide range of economic and social policy, combining our core purpose with a commitment to analytical rigour. These twin pillars of rigour and purpose underpin everything we do and make us the leading UK authority on securing widely-shared economic growth. The Foundation's established work programme includes incomes and inequality; jobs, skills and pay; housing, wealth and debt; tax and welfare; public finances and the economy.

Centre for Economic Performance

The Centre for Economic Performance (CEP) at the London School of Economics and Political Science (LSE) carries out policy-focused research on the causes of economic growth and effective ways to create a fair, inclusive and sustainable society. Established at LSE in 1990, CEP is one of Europe's leading economic research centres. It addresses two main questions: How to improve economic performance, and how to share the gains of this growth in a fair, inclusive and sustainable way? Research at the Centre tackles a wide range of subjects with a focus on informing public policy. Our work covers six broad areas: community wellbeing, education and skills, economic growth, labour markets, trade, and urban economics.

The Nuffield Foundation

The Nuffield Foundation is an independent charitable trust with a mission to advance social well-being. It funds research that informs social policy, primarily in Education, Welfare, and Justice. It also funds student programmes that provide opportunities for young people to develop skills in quantitative and scientific methods. The Nuffield Foundation is the founder and co-funder of the Nuffield Council on Bioethics, the Nuffield Family Justice Observatory and the Ada Lovelace Institute. The Foundation has funded this project, but the views expressed are those of the authors and not necessarily the Foundation. Visit www.nuffieldfoundation.org.